National Gallery of Ireland

Fifty Irish Portraits

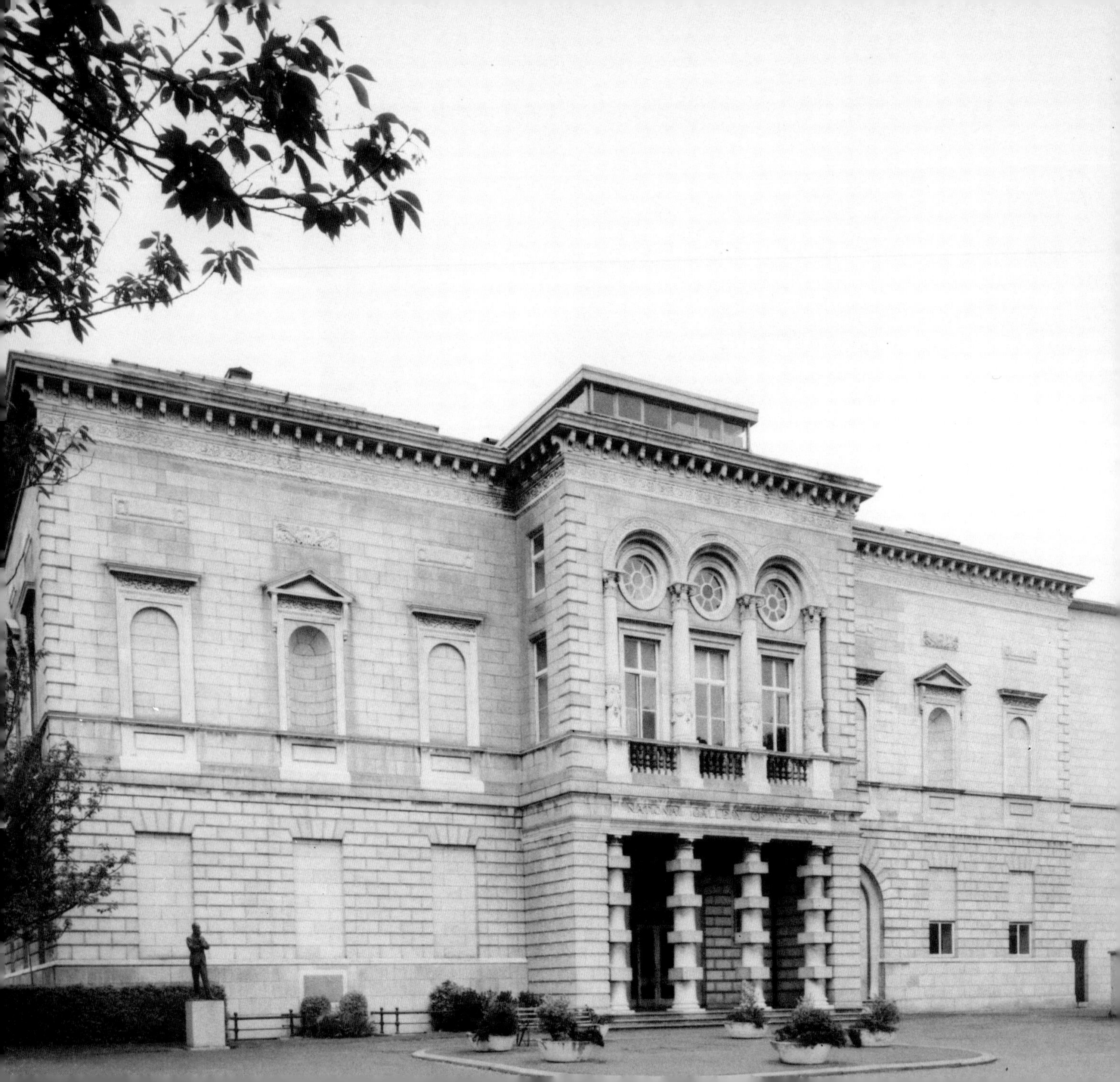

National Gallery of Ireland

Fifty Irish Portraits

by Ann Stewart

The National Gallery of Ireland 1984

The publication of *Fifty Irish Portraits*
has been made possible through the
generous gift of
Mr William Roth.

British Library Cataloguing in Publication Data

National Gallery of Ireland
    National Gallery of Ireland : fifty Irish
    portraits.
    1. Ireland—Biography—Portraits—Catalogs
    I. Title   II. Stewart, Ann, 19--
    704.9'42   N7600

    ISBN 0-903162-13-X

First published, 1984, by the National Gallery of Ireland,
Merrion Square, Dublin 2.

Edited by Joanna Mitchel
Photography by Declan Emerson
Design, origination and print production by Printset & Design Ltd., Dublin
Printed in Ireland by Ormond Printing Company Limited, Dublin.

FOREWORD

The National Gallery of Ireland, which was established by Act of Parliament in 1854, was conceived primarily as an Old Master Gallery. Within a few years of its opening in 1864, however, the Gallery gradually began to acquire some paintings by Irish artists, but it was not until 1872 that the idea of developing a National Portrait Collection took root. The impetus came from a loan exhibition of National Portraits which was held in Dublin in 1872. That Exhibition contained six hundred and thirty portraits of famous Irishmen and women which had been borrowed largely from private collections in Ireland. Included were the portraits of Sarsfield, Mary Tighe and William Carleton (pages 7, 17 and 32) which had been lent respectively by Lord Talbot de Malahide, Lady Laura Grattan and Mrs Carleton. After the close of the Exhibition, the Director of the National Gallery of Ireland, Henry Doyle, proposed to the Governors and Guardians of the Gallery that a permanent collection of National Portraits should be established, and he applied to the Treasury for a Grant of £2,000 to purchase portraits of 'personages, either Irish by birth or connected with the public transactions of Ireland'. His request was refused on the grounds that a National Portrait Gallery already existed in London 'where eminent Irishmen were represented indiscriminately with Englishmen and Scotchmen'. Doyle was, nevertheless, not deterred and in the 1875 Catalogue of the Gallery he included a section entitled 'National, Historical and Portrait Collection' which contained twenty-one oil paintings and a number of busts, drawings and engravings. Among the paintings were the portraits of Lady Morgan (page 25), the Duke of Ormonde (page 5), Samuel Lover (page 30), the Duke of Wellington (page 21) and Sir Thomas Wyse (page 29). Since that time the collection of National Portraits in the National Gallery of Ireland has grown extensively and most Irish people of note from the late sixteenth century to the present day are represented. It is from this

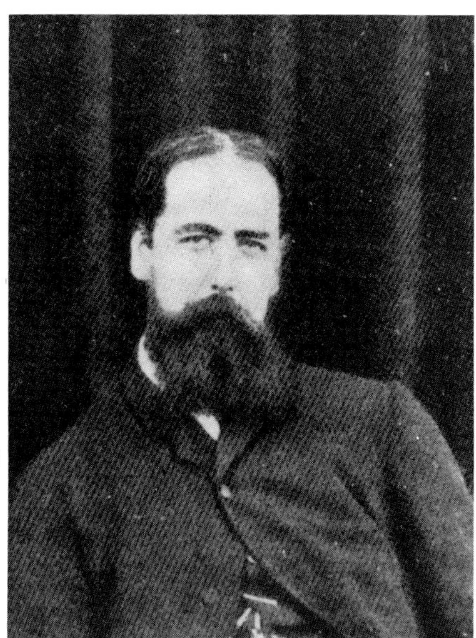

Henry Doyle 1827-1892 Director of the National Gallery 1869-1892. He initiated the collection of National Portraits in 1872.

collection that fifty portraits have been selected for inclusion in this book.

The Irish are more generally renowned for the eloquence of their tongues than for the allure of their appearance, although the latter aspect has not infrequently been commented upon. Queen Victoria, on a visit to Cork in 1849, thought 'the beauty of the women very remarkable' and a century earlier in 1746 when Arthur Young made his *Tour in Ireland* he found 'fewer people of a disagreeable countenance than any part where I have been'. He described the people as 'rather tall than low, strong and active and both sexes generally handsome. They excel in most bodily exercises, endure fatigue of all kinds with great patience, and are satisfied with very sparing food. They are of ready wit; the ridiculous notion we have of their stupidity is the worst grounded in the world'. The publication in this book of fifty portraits of Irish people will allow the reader to assess the accuracy of Young's remarks.

The portraits, which have been selected and are described by Ann Stewart, include paintings of those who were famous for their beauty like The Fair Geraldine (page 1), Maria Gunning (page 15) and Lady Lavery (page 49); those who were witty like Jonathan Swift (page 8), George Moore (page 43) and George Bernard Shaw (page 45); those who were dissolute like Sterne (page 11), Lady Blessington (page 26) · and William Wallace (page 38); those who were learned like Luke Wadding (page 4), Berkeley (page 10) and Burke (page 13); and those who achieved notoriety like Parnell (page 42), Lady Wilde (page 41) and James Joyce (page 46). As regards the Irishness of the people represented, some, like Nellie Farren (page 20), were born in Ireland but achieved distinction abroad; others like Gandon (page 16) were born abroad but found fame in Ireland. Some, like Lawrence of Arabia (page 50), were born abroad of Irish parents and others, like Lady Lavery (page 49), were Irish by adoption. Ann Stewart includes them all and those who are excluded, are so only through lack of space. For that reason alone Robert Boyle the chemist is not here: he has not been excluded because of his rude remark that he was 'Irish by birth but not by ancestry, residence or inclination'. Ignoring such impertinences, Ann Stewart has included for example the Duke of Wellington (page 21) and quotes his famous remark about horses and stables. Her biographies, however, are not limited to anecdote alone as in the small space available she manages to adeptly convey the historical setting in which those represented lived. Her book is a visual history of Ireland from the late sixteenth to the early twentieth century and by including short biographies of the artists she traces the story of portrait painting in Ireland.

Fifty Irish Portraits is intended to be enjoyed by a wide public. By means of the colour illustrations and the obvious enjoyment with which Ann Stewart has described them, I hope it will lead to a wider appreciation of the National Gallery of Ireland's National Portrait Collection.

HOMAN POTTERTON
Director, The National Gallery of Ireland

'Her Sire an Earl, her dame of
   Princess blood,
From tender years, in Britain she
   doth rest,
With kinges child . . .'

Thus was Elizabeth Fitzgerald, 'The Fair Geraldine' immortalized in the poetry of Henry Howard, Earl of Surrey. Born at Maynooth Castle, stronghold of her father, Garret Óg, ninth Earl of Kildare, Elizabeth was cousin to King Henry VIII through her mother. After the ill-fated rebellion of her half-brother, Silken Thomas, Elizabeth was taken to England and placed in the household of her kinswoman, the Princess Mary. She never returned to Ireland where the power of the Fitzgeralds was effectively broken, but remained at court until married off to a trusted companion of the King. On her second marriage in 1552 she became Countess of Lincoln.

Although Elizabeth was only ten years old when the Earl of Surrey first met her, he wrote a series of songs and sonnets extolling her beauty, and made her the object of his 'courtly love', until his tragic death on the scaffold. Later poets took up this story, inventing a mythical descent from Dante for the Fitzgeralds. The poet Michael Drayton first referred to this in his *Heroicall Epistles* and three centuries later Sir Walter Scott again took up the story in his *Lay of the Last Minstrel*.

This portrait was painted around 1560 when Elizabeth was Countess of Lincoln, and for a long time it was confused with a portrait of her step-daughter, but the famous red hair of the Geraldines finally identifies her, 'Bright is her hue, and Geraldine she Hight'. The painting remained for several centuries at Woburn Abbey in the collection of the Dukes of Bedford and is one of the few existing portraits of a 16th century Irish noblewoman.

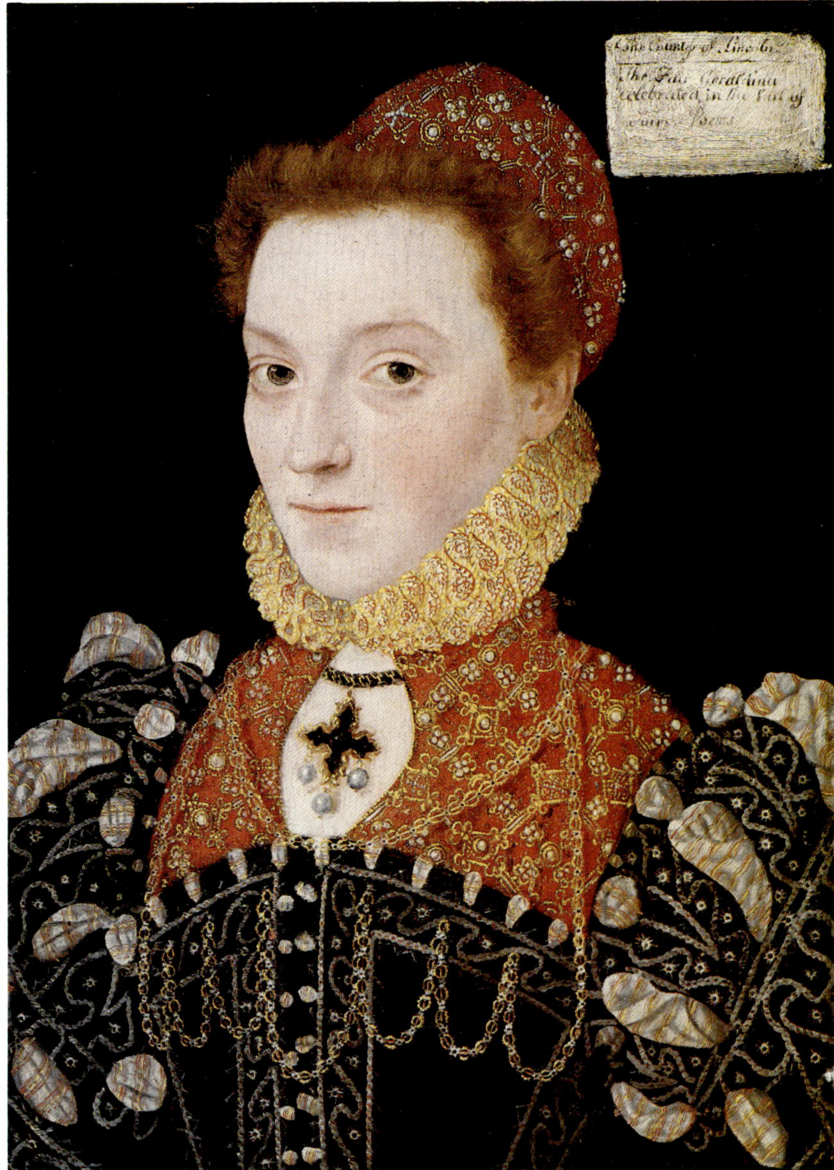

English School 16th Century
Portrait of **ELIZABETH FITZGERALD,** c.1528-1589
'The Fair Geraldine'
Oil on panel, 46 x 34 cms. Purchased, 1950

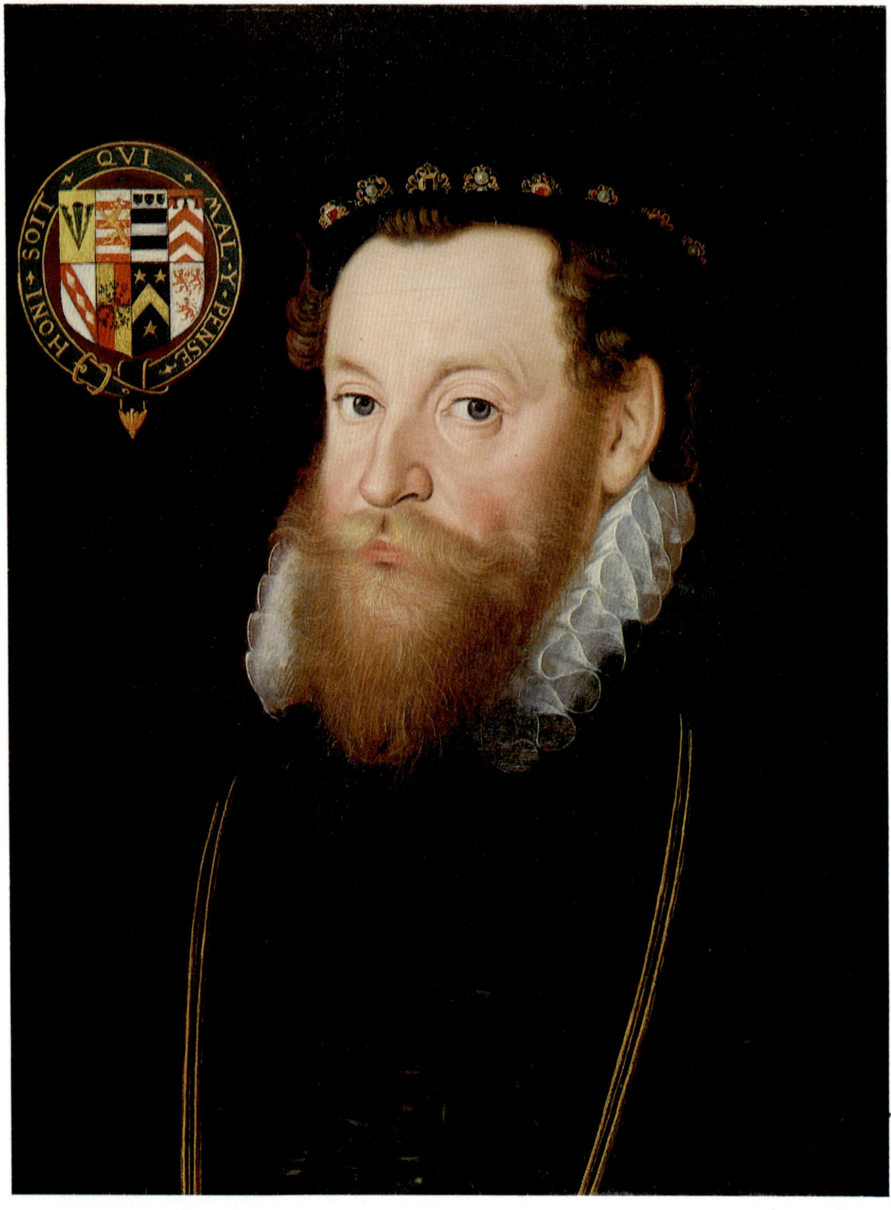

English School 16th Century
Portrait of **SIR HENRY SIDNEY**, 1529-1586, Lord Deputy of Ireland
Oil on panel, 58 x 48 cms. Purchased, 1926

One of England's most successful Lord Deputies of Ireland, Sir Henry Sidney grew up at the English court as companion to the young Edward VI. He survived the vagaries of the Tudor Succession despite marriage to a daughter of the Earl of Northumberland, the Tudor 'Kingmaker', and managed to retain the favour of both Queen Mary and Queen Elizabeth. He was appointed Lord Deputy of Ireland in 1665 and over the next twenty years his terms in this office went a long way towards consolidating the English presence in Ireland. He rebuilt Dublin Castle and Shannon Bridge and restored Strongbow's Tomb. His son, the poet Sir Philip Sidney, spent part of his youth in Ireland and Edmund Spenser first came to Ireland to carry despatches between Sidney and his brother-in-law, the Earl of Leicester.

Sidney's success might have been greater had the English Crown had a better understanding of his effectiveness. Despite Shane O'Neill's Ulster Wars, the Ormonde/Geraldine disputes in the South and Grace O'Malley in Connaught, Sidney still managed to extend English law to most of the country. However he had to contend not only with the warring Irish but with court intrigue in London, where faction fought faction for the Queen's favour and usually Sidney ended up being recalled in disgrace for a few years. His final recall was for alienating the loyal Pale with demands for money to support his military campaigns. He died at Ludlow Castle before Elizabeth could again appoint him Lord Deputy.

The early origins of this painting remain something of a mystery, as does the identity of the artist. It is, however, a very fine portrait and shows Sidney with the family coat of arms in the top left hand corner encircled by the Order of the Garter.

Born in Devon, Sir Walter Raleigh spent his early years seeking his fortune as a mercenary. He fought in the Desmond wars in Munster, did garrison duty in Cork, and was granted 12,000 acres of rich land in the area for his services. Sent to London with despatches, Raleigh attracted the notice of Queen Elizabeth and he was made Captain of the Queen's Guard. He financed several expeditions to the New World and was responsible for the first English settlement in Virginia and the introduction of tobacco and potatoes to Europe. His secret marriage to Bess Throckmorton ended his reign as the Queen's favourite. In 1603, Raleigh was condemned to death for treason against King James. He spent the next twelve years imprisoned in the Tower of London, occupying himself with the study of science and literature and writing his *History of the World.* He was released to sail on a final expedition to South America and, on his return without the fabulous gold he had promised to the King, Raleigh was finally beheaded.

During his years of power Raleigh acquired some 40,000 acres of land in Cork, Tipperary and Wexford. He settled these lands with men from his native Devon and is reputed to have grown the first potatoes in Europe in his gardens at Youghal. In 1604, in trouble with King James and in dire need of money, Raleigh sold his vast Irish lands for the nominal sum of £1,000 to anther English adventurer, Richard Boyle, later first Earl of Cork.

This late portrait of Raleigh shows him wearing a jerkin described by a contemporary as 'beset with jewels to the value of threescore thousand pounds'. In the top left hand corner a map of Cadiz refers to his greatest sea victory, when he boldly sailed into Cadiz harbour and stormed the city.

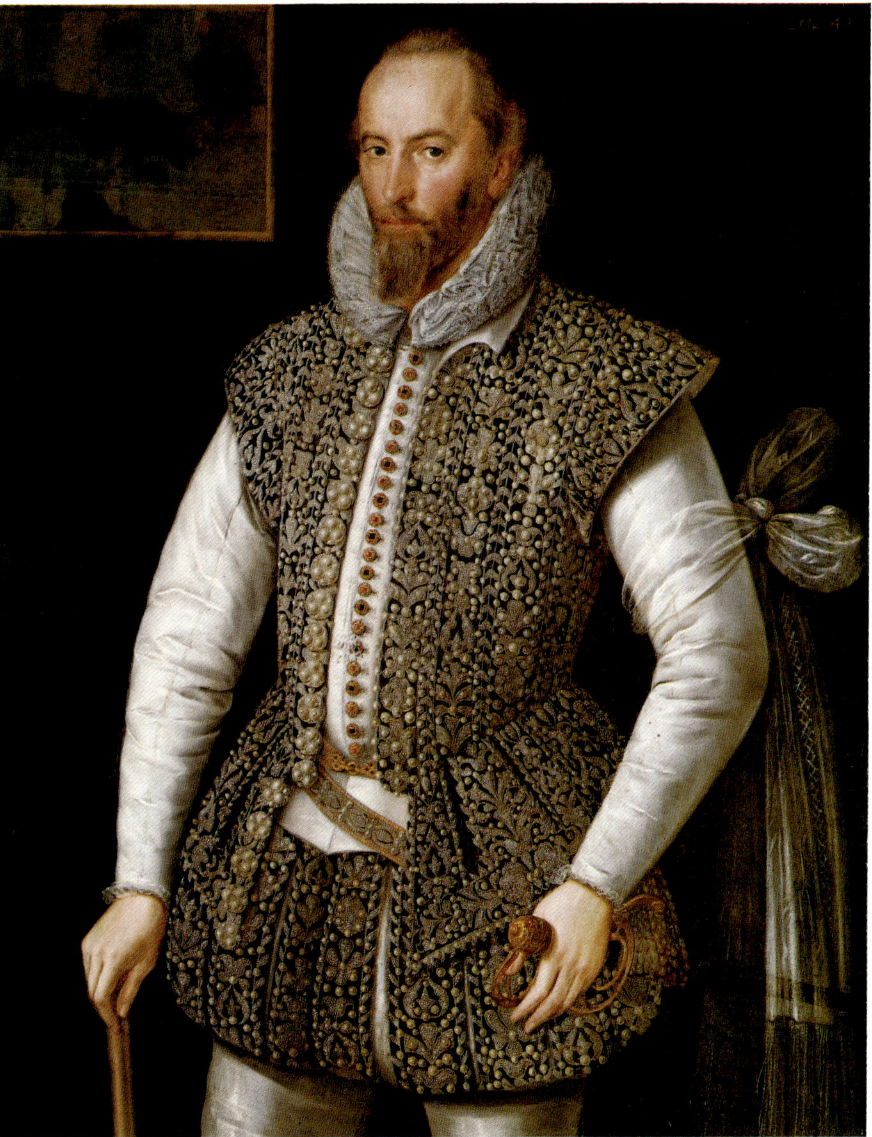

English School, 16th Century
Portrait of **SIR WALTER RALEIGH,** 1552-1618, Soldier and Explorer
Dated: *1598.* Oil on canvas, 109 x 84 cms. Purchased, 1887.

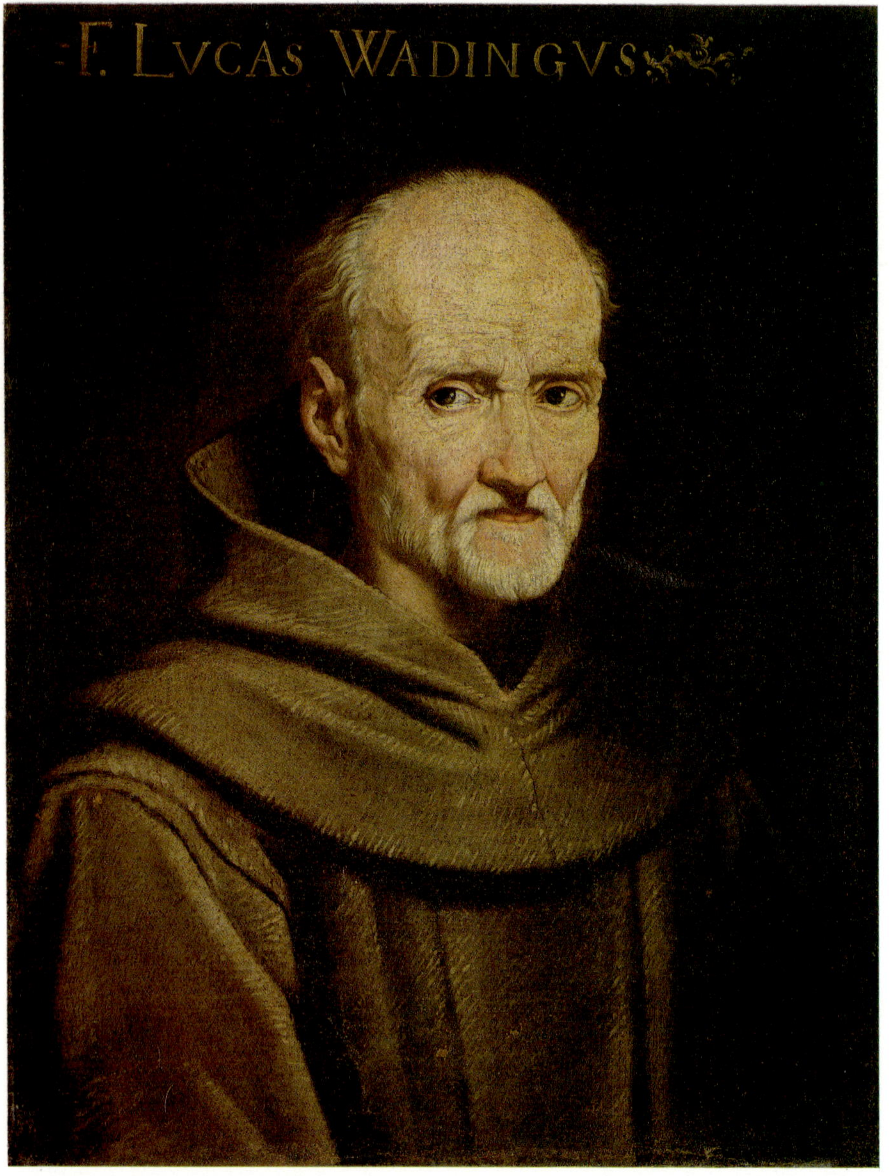

Luke Wadding was born in Waterford and was sent to study in Spain as a youth in order to avoid the anti-Catholic laws in Ireland. He entered the Franciscan Order there and for a time became President of the Irish College at Salamanca. He was sent to Rome as part of a Spanish emissary to debate the doctrine of the Immaculate Conception, and remained there to become a powerful figure in the Church and in the cultural life of Rome. He founded the Irish College of St. Isidore's in Rome and wrote many scholarly works including the eighteen volume History of the Franciscan Order and a twelve volume edition of the works of Duns Scotus. He amassed a library of over five thousand books which he left to the College. He was a keen collector of Irish books and manuscripts and when the library of St. Isidore's was removed for safe-keeping to Ireland in 1870, one of the most important early collections of Irish manuscripts was returned to its native soil.

The Irish Franciscan never forgot the country of his birth and the plight of his fellow Catholics there. He was advisor and friend to Owen Roe O'Neill and closely followed the progress of the Confederation Wars of 1641 onwards. He advised the Pope to send Rinuccini to Ireland, approached Richelieu for support and personally raised money to send arms and officers to bolster O'Neill's army. His influence on the Vatican's understanding of Irish affairs lasted for centuries after his death until even Gladstone in the 19th century blamed St. Isidore's for the Vatican's anti-English bias in Irish affairs.

The Gallery's portrait of Wadding is a copy of one by the Roman artist Carlo Maratti, painted in 1652 the year Maratti was commissioned to paint the Alaleona Chapel of St. Isidore's. Maratti also supplied drawings of Wadding for engravings.

After Carlo Maratti, 1625-1713
Portrait of **FATHER LUKE WADDING,** 1588-1657,
Franciscan Scholar
Oil on canvas, 66 x 51 cms. Purchased, 1889.

James Butler was born in London and was only nine when his father's death left him heir to one of the greatest Irish families. He became a royal ward and, although the Butlers were traditionally Catholic, he was educated as a Protestant and remained loyal to this religion all his life. He married a cousin, heiress to the Earl of Desmond, thus reuniting the estranged branches of the Butler family, and by the age of 23 he was Earl of Ormonde and Ossery and the most powerful peer in Ireland.

Thomas Strafford, Earl of Wentworth, during his term as King's Representative in Ireland recognised Ormonde's influence with the Irish and took care to befriend him. During the 1641 rebellion Ormonde was commander-in-chief of the King's army and was Rinuccini's main antagonist. He continued to uphold the crown until defeated and driven from the country by Cromwell's forces. He remained in exile during the Commonwealth, negotiating the return of Charles II. After the Restoration Charles rewarded him with the offices of Lord High Steward of England and Lord Deputy of Ireland, and made him 1st Duke of Ormonde. He was one of the few nobles to know of Charles' secret Catholicism and, although he disapproved of this, he served the king loyally, only retiring from public office on the succession of James II.

Lely was a Dutch artist who settled in England where he became a successful portrait painter. He painted Charles I and his family in captivity and after the Restoration he succeeded Van Dyck as Court painter to Charles II. More than any other artist he depicted the life and personages of the Restoration Court. The Ormonde portrait is typical of his style and shows the Duke dressed in the Robes of the Garter and holding the wand of the Lord High Steward.

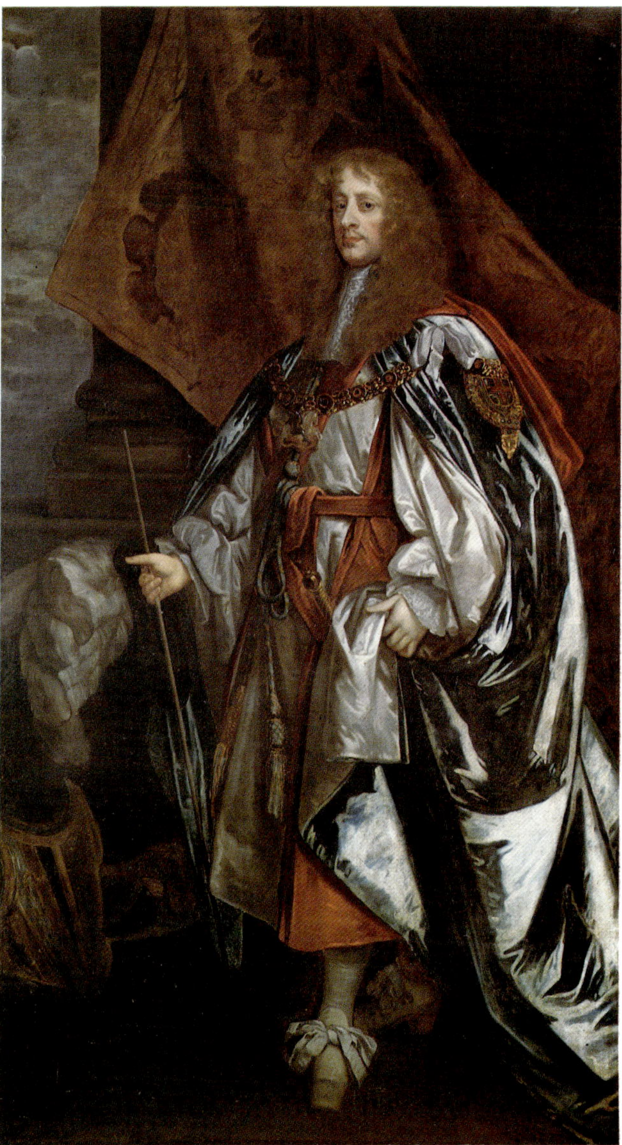

Peter Lely, 1618-1680
Portrait of **JAMES BUTLER,** 1st. Duke of Ormonde, 1610-1688, Statesman
Oil on canvas, 229 x 132 cms.
Presented by the 7th Earl of Carlisle, 1864

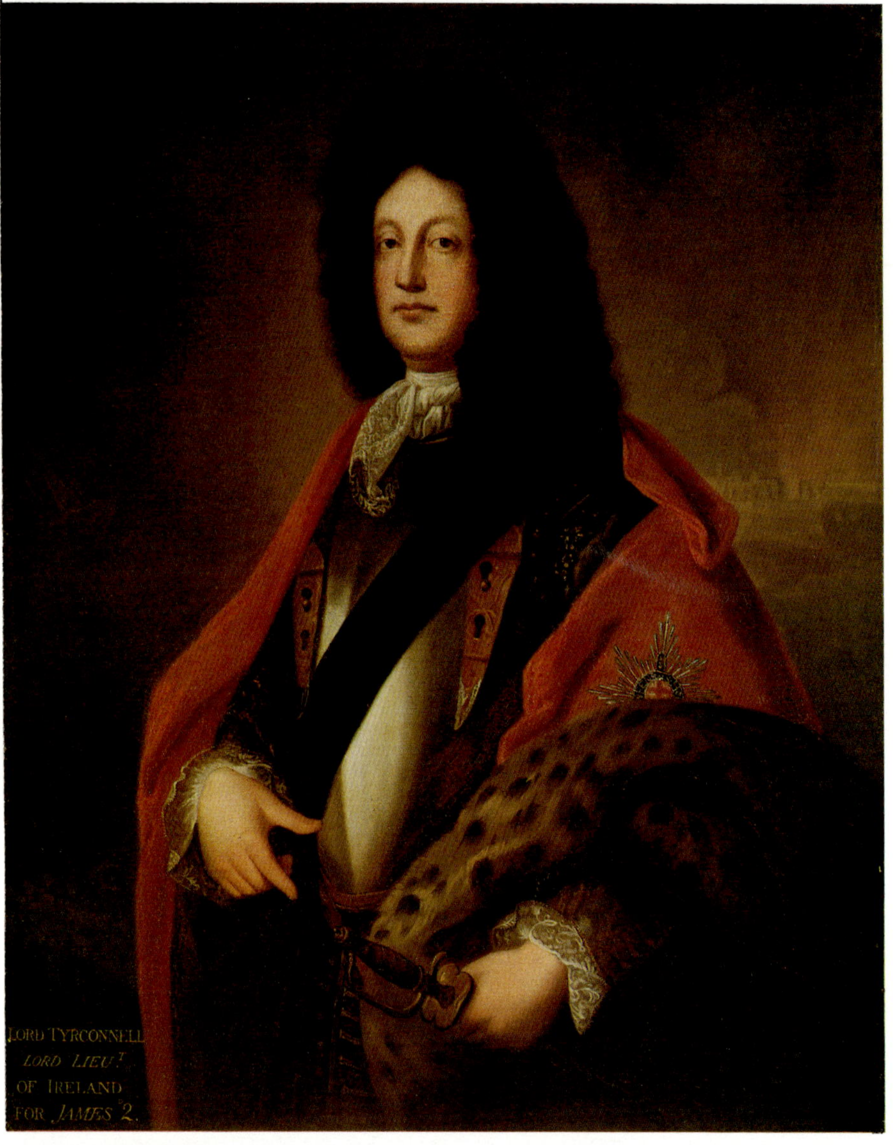

English School, 17th Century
Portrait of **RICHARD TALBOT,** Earl and Titular Duke of Tyrconnell,
1630-1691, Soldier
Oil on canvas, 118 x 91 cms. Purchased, 1976.

Richard Talbot was born in Malahide, County Dublin and spent his youth fighting in the Irish wars of the 1640's. He supported the Duke of Ormonde (q.v.) against Rinuccini and was wounded in the defence of Drogheda during Cromwell's seige. In exile on the Continent, he fought in Spain and Flanders before joining the household of James, Duke of York. He returned to London with James after the Restoration. As a Catholic whose sympathies lay with those Irish who had suffered dispossession during the Commonwealth, Talbot came frequently into conflict with the Duke of Ormonde who represented the opposite side in Irish politics. Ormonde had the protection of King Charles, and Talbot was sent to the Tower on several occasions for his quarrels with the powerful Duke.

With the succession of James II, Talbot was created Earl of Tyrconnell and given the task of raising a loyal force in Ireland for the King. This he did by the simple expedient of expelling Protestants from the army and replacing them with untrained Catholics. The result was the complete alienation of the Protestant community from James. Talbot also sent the garrison of Derry to England leaving the way open for the Apprentice Boys to man the walls against seige by James, and he was made the butt of the anti-Catholic ballad *Lillibulero.* He was commander at the Battle of the Boyne and afterwards advised James to leave the country. He died during the seige of Limerick and was buried in an unmarked tomb in Limerick Cathedral.

The portrait of Tyrconnell was probably a copy of a miniature by Petitot owned by the Talbot family and was in the family collection at Malahide Castle until purchased by the Gallery at the sale of this collection in 1976.

Patrick Sarsfield was born into an Anglo-Irish Catholic family with ties of loyalty to the English crown, while through his mother he could also claim descent from the Gaelic leader Rory O'More. He was educated at a French military academy and later took service with James II as a Life Guard. When James decided to raise an Irish force to help his weakening position in England, Sarsfield was given a command and soon cleared Connaught of King William's supporters.

During the Williamite Wars in Ireland, Sarsfield played an increasingly important role, not least because of his great popularity with the troops. He defended Limerick during the seige of 1690 and there made his heroic attempt to capture William of Orange in the famous ambush at Ballyneety. After the disastrous defeat at Aughrim and the death of St. Ruth, it was Sarsfield who gathered the remnants of the Irish together and retreated to Limerick. He became commander-in-chief of the Irish army after the death of Tyrconnell and was forced to negotiate the Treaty of Limerick in 1691 which allowed the Irish to choose between service in the English army or exile. Along with 19,000 of his soldiers Sarsfield chose exile and confiscation of his lands rather than submit to King William. Two years later he was mortally wounded at the battle of Lunden in the Netherlands, and seeing his life blood flow away was heard to lament 'Ah! If this were for Ireland.'

Few portraits of Sarsfield exist and there is little record of his appearance. The present portrait came from the Talbot family collection at Malahide, and resembles one other named portrait of him owned by the Franciscan Order in Ireland.

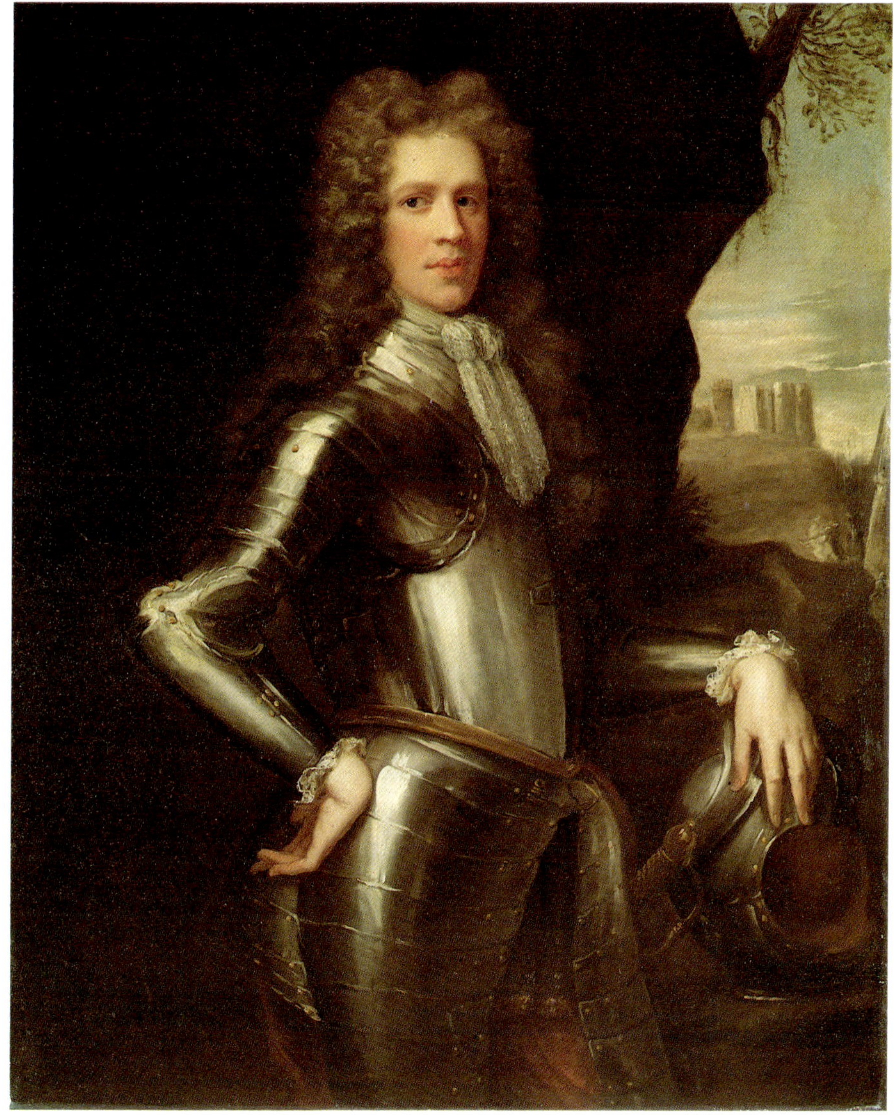

John Riley, 1646-1691 Attributed to
Portrait of **PATRICK SARSFIELD,** d.1693, Soldier
Oil on canvas, 124 x 102 cms. Purchased, 1976

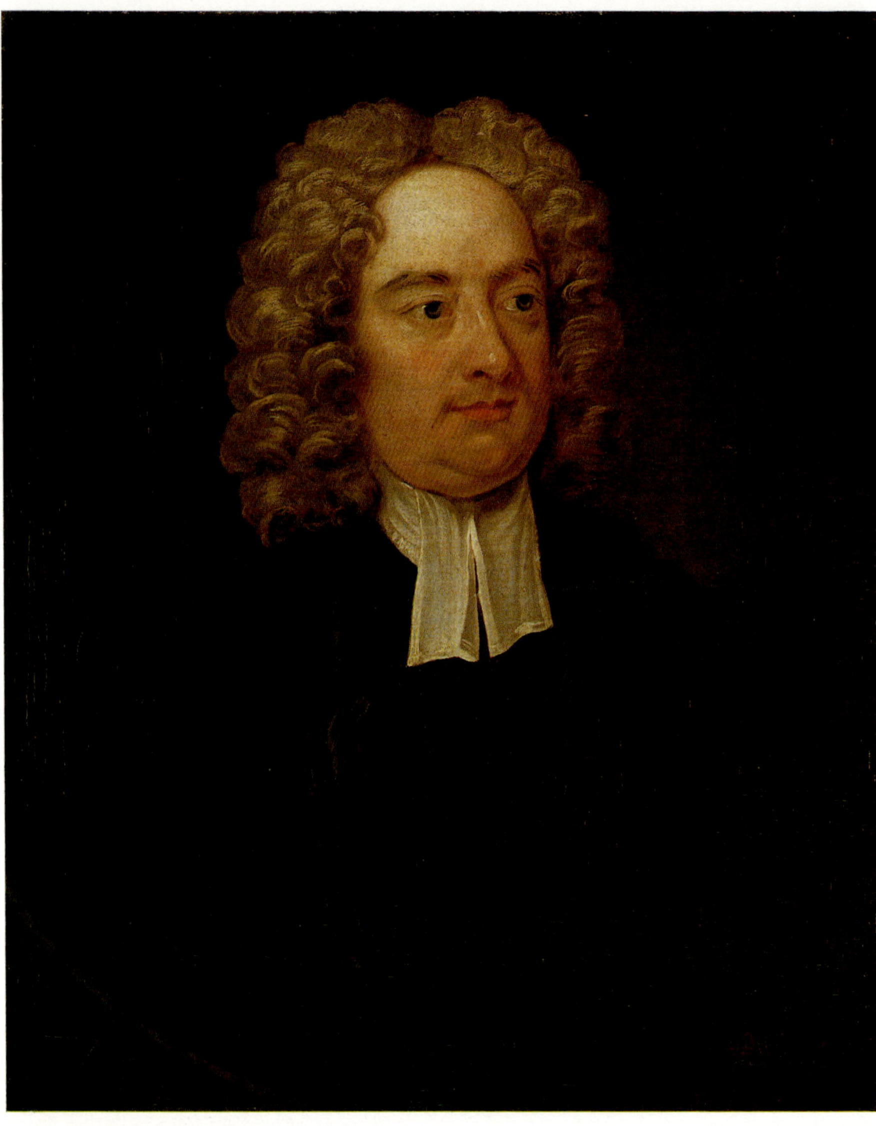

Charles Jervas, c.1675-1739
Portrait of **JONATHAN SWIFT**, 1667-1745, Satirist
Oil on canvas, 74 x 62 cms. Purchased, 1875

Jonathan Swift was born in Dublin and after an undistinguished career at Trinity College found employment as secretary to the English politician Sir William Temple at Moor Park, Surrey. To further his career Swift took Holy Orders, but spent little time on his Irish livings, preferring to visit London where his Tory friends put his brilliant and acerbic pen to work writing political pamphlets and anti-Whig lampoons. Swift's reward for this was not the bishopric he had hoped for, but exile, as he considered it, to Dublin as Dean of St. Patrick's Cathedral. Here Swift wrote his most famous satire on society, *Gulliver's Travels* and, as he became increasingly disillusioned with England's mismanagement of Ireland, he turned again to pamphleteering with the Drapier letters. His final years were haunted by a fear of encroaching insanity.

Swift's relationship with two women, Stella and Vanessa, remains shrouded in mystery. He first met Hester Johnson, better known as Stella, at Moor Park. When Swift moved to his living at Laracor, County Meath, Stella moved to live nearby and from London Swift wrote her his *Journals to Stella.* It is generally believed they were secretly married. Vanessa, or Esther Vanhomrigh, was an Irish heiress who pursued Swift for many years to his great embarrassment. They finally quarrelled over his relationship with Stella and Vanessa died of a broken heart.

Charles Jervas was an Irish artist who studied in Italy and was a pupil of Kneller, whom he succeeded as principal painter to the King. Jervas painted Swift many times and the Dean learned to avoid him when he came to Dublin. 'Do you hear anything of Jervas going?' he wrote to a friend in 1716, 'for I hate to be in town when he is there'.

Although born in England, William Congreve was brought up in Ireland where his father was estate agent to the Great Earl of Cork. He attended Kilkenny College with Swift (q.v.) and later, at Trinity College, Dublin, they became close friends. Sent to London to continue his law studies, Congreve found the world of literature more to his taste and began to write seriously. After an attempt at an unremarkable novel he achieved immediate success with his first play *The Old Batchelor,* produced at Drury Lane in 1693.

A few more plays quickly established Congreve as the leading exponent of Restoration comedy of manners. By the age of thirty he had written the five plays on which his dramatic reputation is based. But tastes were changing as the Stuart age drew to a close, and his plays were considered outdated and immoral by many. Congreve himself became wealthy and lazy, more concerned with being known as a gentleman than an author. When *The Way of the World* was coldly received in 1700, he resolved to write no more plays and retired to live on the revenue of some Government sinecures. He died in 1729 and was buried with great pomp in Westminster Abbey.

Geoffrey Kneller was then the leading English portrait painter, his style influencing artists for almost a century. This portrait of Congreve is identical to that in Kneller's famous series of Kit Cat members, now in the National Portrait Gallery, London, and observes the Kit Cat format of showing the sitter's head and shoulders with one hand in view.

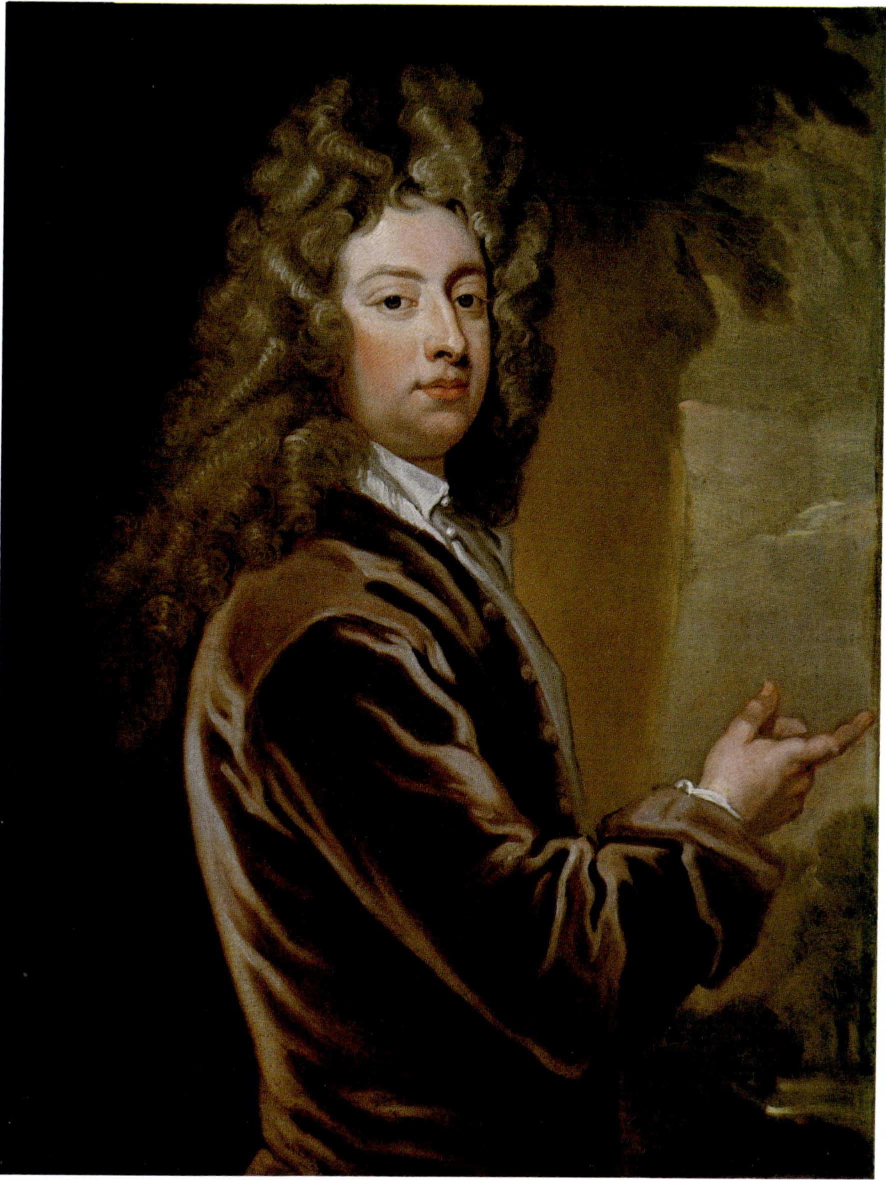

Sir Godfrey Kneller, 1646-1723
Portrait of **WILLIAM CONGREVE**, 1671-1729, Dramatist
Oil on canvas, 90 x 35 cms. Presented by Mr. John Chambers, 1980

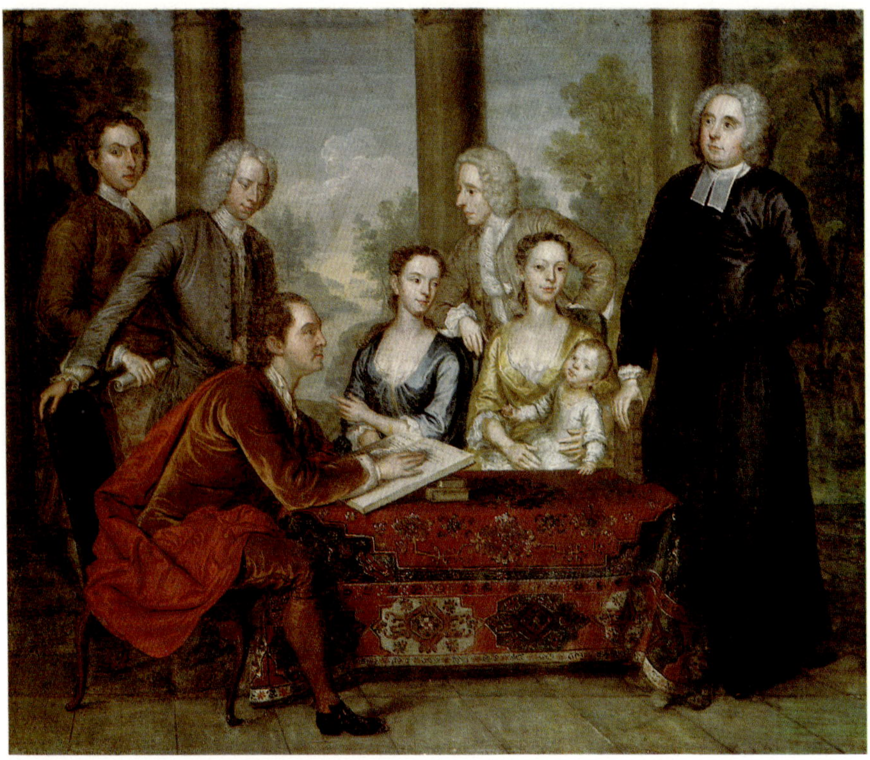

John Smibert, 1688-1751
Portrait of **GEORGE BERKELEY**, 1685-1753, Philosopher. With his
Wife and Friends. Right to left: Bishop Berkeley, Mrs Berkeley and son
Henry, John James of Bury St. Edmunds, Miss Hancock, Richard
Dalton, Dr. Thomas Moffat, (Smibert's nephew) and John Smibert.
Oil on canvas, 61 x 70 cms. Purchased, 1897

George Berkeley was born near Thomastown, County Kilkenny and attended Trinity College, Dublin, where he became a fellow and took Holy Orders. His brilliant philosophical writings earned him a reputation as a metaphysist and visionary. He became disillusioned with the 'moral decline' of society and conceived a plan to found a College in Bermuda for the education of clergymen which would ensure the propagation of pure Christianity in the New World and the conversion of the 'Savage American'.

Berkeley acquired a Charter for the College and with the promise of financial assistance to follow, he married and sailed to Newport, Rhode Island, in 1728. The promised money never arrived and after four years of waiting, Berkeley abandoned the project and returned to Europe. He left behind a collection of books and property to endow scholarships for Yale University. He retired to his Irish bishopric of Cloyne and devoted his later years to family, metaphysics, and empirical medicine. His last great cause was an American Indian medicine called Tar-Water, which he advocated to all as a panacea for every physical and moral ill.

Smibert was a Scottish artist who studied under Kneller and in Italy. Berkeley invited him to become Professor of Architecture in the Bermuda College and, when the venture failed, Smibert settled in Boston and became an influential portrait painter. This picture is a study for a larger painting which is now in Yale. The larger work excited much interest as one of the earliest conversation pieces painted in the Colony and remained on view in Smibert's studio throughout his life. The study was probably painted for the artist's nephew and was purchased by the Gallery from his descendants.

Laurence Sterne was born in Clonmel, County Tipperary, where his father, an officer in the English Army, was stationed. His mother was Irish and as his father moved from garrison to garrison, Sterne picked up the rudiments of an education from his Irish relatives before being sent to school in England. Later, at Cambridge, he took Holy Orders and, through the good offices of an uncle, received a living close to York City and there he remained most of his life. As a vicar he was not an outstanding success being a bad preacher, unpopular with his parishioners and unfaithful to his wife, driving her to insanity. In desperation Sterne took to writing and produced his eccentric books, *Tristram Shandy* and *A Sentimental Journey* as well as carrying on voluminous correspondence with several lady friends.

Sterne might have been the most unlikely vicar ever to have been inflicted on a parish, but his whimsical, bawdy and semi-autobiographical depiction of the Rev. Yorick has ensured him immortality. With the publication of *Tristram Shandy* he became an overnight celebrity, fêted in London where he shocked and amused in turn, while his parishioners became completely alienated. They agreed with the judgement of some of the wits, Goldsmith, Johnson and Walpole, who considered his writing immoral and in bad taste.

Reynolds painted Sterne several times and this is a copy of one of these portraits. Of the original Mrs. Jameson the critic wrote, 'the subtle evanescent expression of satire round the lips, the shrewd significance in the eye, the earnest contemplative attitude, all convey the strongest impression of the man, and of his peculiar genius and peculiar humour'.

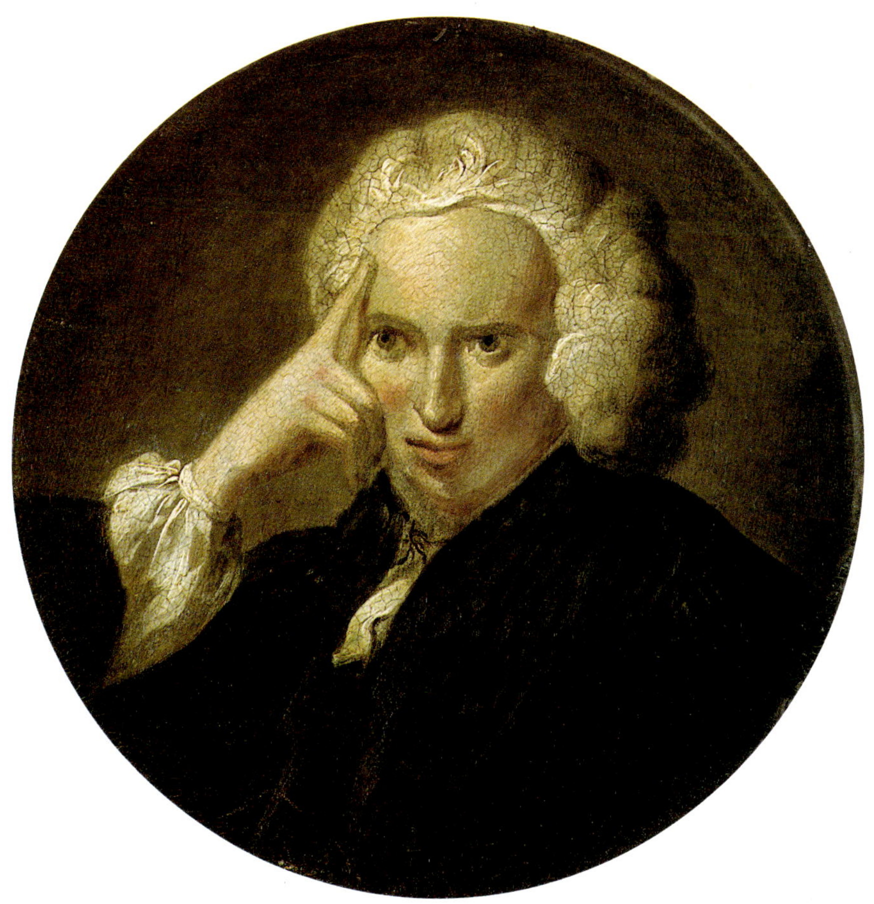

Robert West, c.1749-1809, (after Reynolds)
Portrait of **LAURENCE STERNE,** 1713-1768, Author
Oil on metal, dia. 27 cms. Purchased, 1887

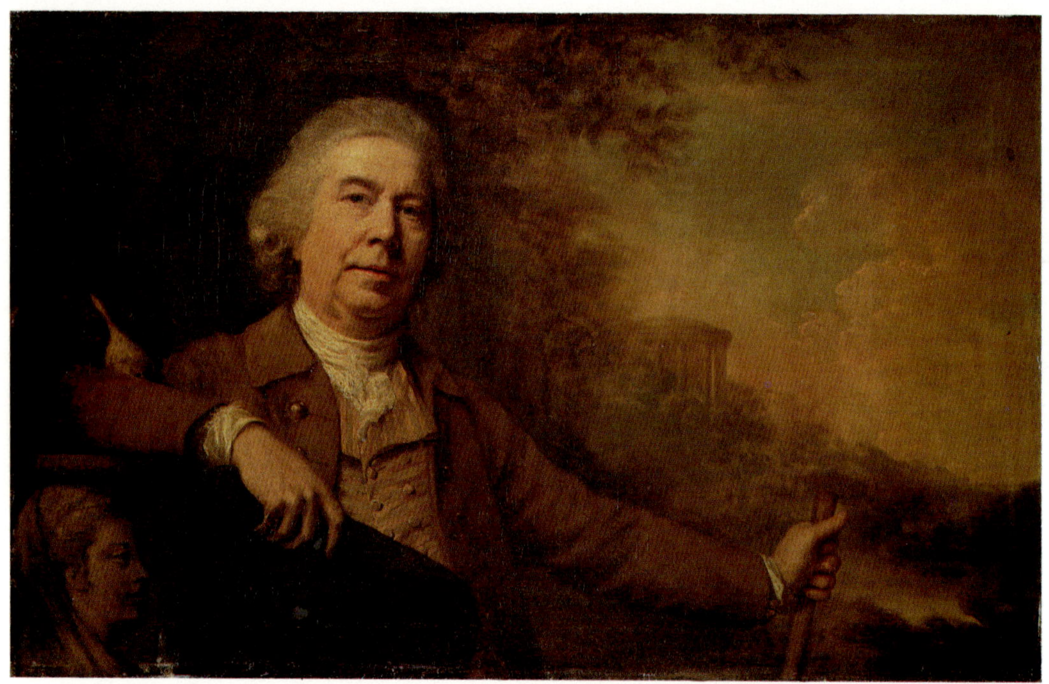

Nathaniel Hone the Elder, 1718-1784, Artist
A SELF-PORTRAIT
Oil on canvas, 76 x 122 cms. Hone Bequest, 1919

Little is known of the early life of Nathaniel Hone save that he was born in Dublin, the son of a merchant from Wood Quay. He spent some years working as an itinerant portrait painter until his marriage to a wealthy Yorkshire woman in 1747 enabled him to settle in London and set up a studio. He worked variously in oil, pastel and engraving, and collected Old Master drawings and prints. He was a founder member of the Royal Academy, but his irascible temperament and jealousy of rival artists made him many enemies; and he was often in trouble with the Academy for trying to exhibit controversial paintings. Several of his children became artists and two important Irish artists, Evie Hone (1894-1955) and Nathaniel Hone the Younger (1831-1917) were family descendants.

In 1775 Hone submitted his most famous painting, *The Pictorial Conjuror displaying the Whole Art of Optical Deception* (now in the National Gallery of Ireland), to the Royal Academy. This painting was a thinly disguised attack on the President of the Academy, Sir Joshua Reynolds, and on his relationship with fellow academician Angelica Kauffman. The painting was promptly rejected by the hanging committee, and Hone made some token attempt to modify the work. This was not enough to satisfy public opinion, however, and in a rage with the Academy, Hone held an alternative exhibition of his own works at his studio in St. Martin's Lane, thus holding the first one man exhibition devoted to the works of a living artist.

Hone painted a series of self-portraits throughout his life, following the model of Rembrandt. Many of these showed his wife somewhere in the painting, often disguised as a portrait or a sculptured head. In this self-portrait Hone paints himself in the pose of a country gentleman complete with dog and walking stick. The Italianate landscape in the background hints at Tivoli and, as usual, his wife appears sculptured in relief on the plinth against which the artist leans.

Irish born and educated, Edmund Burke became one of the greatest English Parliamentarians, a critic of successive Governments and an influential political commentator. He became secretary to Lord Rockingham, served as M.P. for many years and worked closely with Charles James Fox, drafting many of his bills. He foresaw the revolt of the American Colonies and called for greater care in the administration of India and Ireland, lest they also revolt. Always sympathetic to the plight of Ireland, he saw the need for legislative reforms there. He fought a long battle for the impeachment of Warren Hastings and opened the trial with a marathon nine day speech — lengthy even by Irish standards!

As an undergraduate at Trinity College, Dublin, Burke began his *Essay on the Sublime and the Beautiful.* This expressed for the first time the standards of taste and changing sensibility of the age and had great impact on artists and writers of his own and later generations. His *Reflections on the French Revolution* rejected the excesses of the Revolution and branded him as a political conservative. It also provoked Paine to reply with his *Rights of Man,* and ended Burke's long friendship with Fox in a bitter Parliamentary argument which almost ended in a duel.

Burke is shown on the right of this painting, reading his draft of the India Bill to Fox who later carried it through Parliament. Thomas Hickey studied art in Dublin and Italy, and worked for a short time in London. He then went to India where he spent the rest of his life, painting English colonists and Indian nobles, and accompanied Lord McCartney's China mission as official artist.

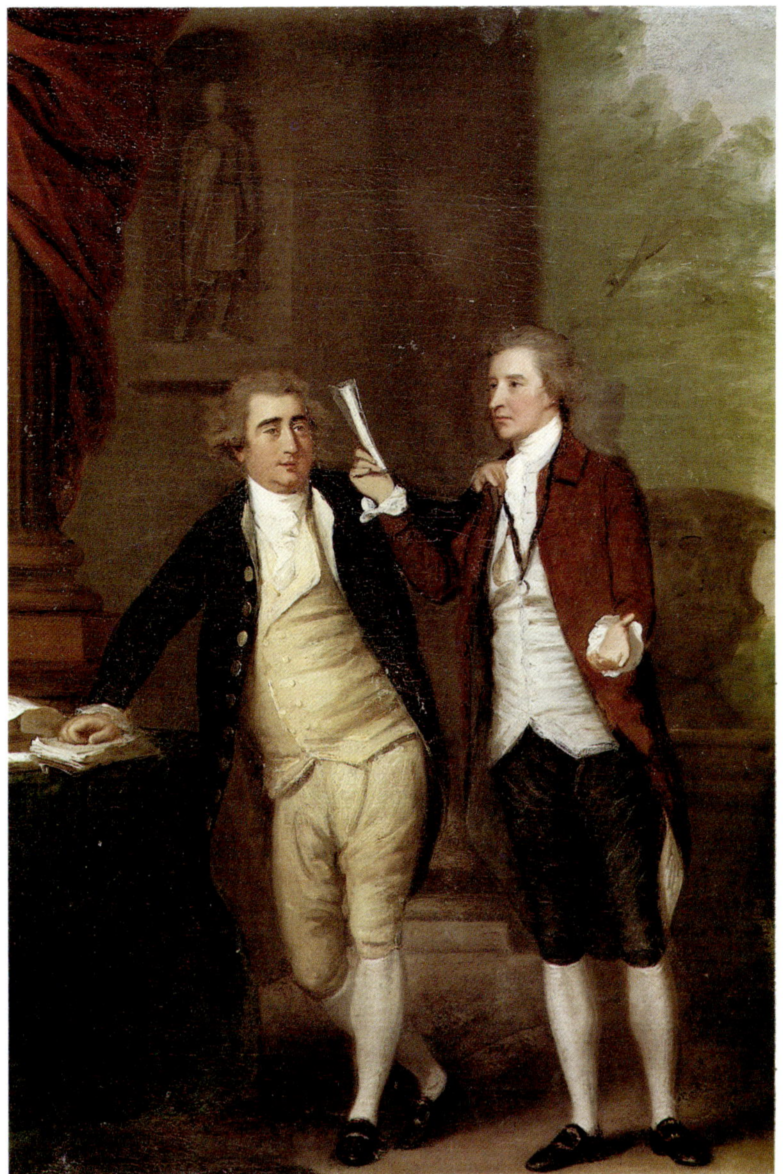

Thomas Hickey, 1741-1824
Portrait of **EDMUND BURKE,** 1729-1797, Politician and Orator.
In Conversation with Charles James Fox.
Oil on canvas, 80 x 59 cms. Purchased, 1886

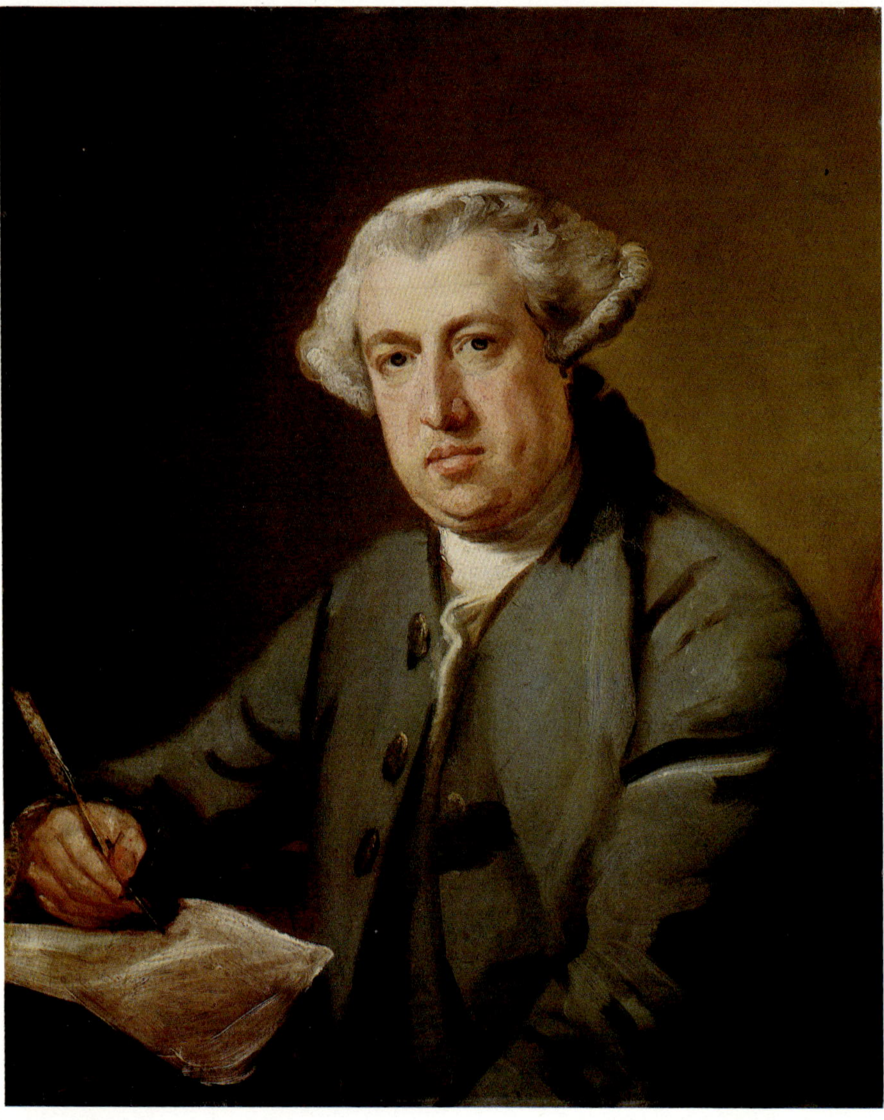

Nathaniel Dance, 1734-1811
Portrait of **ARTHUR MURPHY,** 1727-1805, Actor and Author
Oil on canvas, 76 x 63 cms. Purchased, 1933

Arthur Murphy was born in Clooniquin, County Roscommon, but was brought up in London after his father's death at sea. He was educated at the Jesuit College of St. Omer in France and then an uncle arranged for him to work as a clerk with a Cork merchant firm. This work did not appeal to Murphy and he returned to London to start a weekly paper *The Grey's Inn Journal,* intended to rival the *Spectator.* When his uncle disinherited him, Murphy's theatrical friends persuaded him to try his luck on the stage. This he did with some success and for a time he worked with Garrick, who also produced his first farce. Murphy retired from the stage as soon as he began to write plays, but despite considerable success as a dramatist he attempted to join the Middle Temple. He was refused admission because he had been an actor. Political friends later helped him gain admittance to Lincoln's Inn where he completed his law studies.

Murphy wrote a succession of popular plays; translated and adapted French farces; sometimes drew on Molière for his own plots; wrote tragedies, translated Sallust and Tacitus, and wrote biographies of his friends Garrick and Johnson. Despite this industry, however, he was in financial difficulties by the time he retired from the bar and was granted a pension by George III and made a Commissioner of Bankruptcy.

Nathaniel Dance, one of a family of artists, studied in Italy where be became involved with fellow artist Angelica Kauffman. On his return to England he became a successful portrait painter and a founder member of the Royal Academy. In 1790 he married an heiress and retired from his profession. He took the name Holland-Dance, and entered Parliament where he served as an M.P. for some years.

Maria, Countess of Coventry, was the eldest of the Gunning sisters, the 'Three Graces', whose beauty took London society by storm in 1751. These dowerless daughters of John Gunning of Castlecoote, County Roscommon, at first intended to make their fortunes by going on stage and made their Dublin debut in gowns borrowed from the actress Peg Woffington. Their beauty excited such notice that their ambitious mother took them at once to London in search of wealthy husbands. Before the end of the season Elizabeth married the Duke of Hamilton in a midnight elopement and her sister Maria married the Earl of Coventry three weeks later.

The fashionable beauty of the Gunnings captivated the imagination of the age. They were accorded the sort of adulation reserved today for superstars. Courtiers stood on chairs to see them pass, crowds queued all night, and Maria's daily strolls in Hyde Park were granted a military escort by the King to protect her from the curious. Sadly she did not live long enough to enjoy this adulation, succumbing to consumption at the age of twenty-seven. An affecting account of her last days tells how Lady Coventry 'would not let the bed curtains be open'd, not be look'd at by any mortal but her nurse, she would let no light but a lamp burn in her room lest any see the ravages of her illness'. Ten thousand people came to see her coffin.

Francis Cotes was a struggling young artist when he was commissioned to paint the Gunnings during their first year in London. The portraits were popular and Cotes had them engraved. These engravings sold widely and helped to establish his reputation. He later painted this oil from the original pastel. Maria is seen at the age of eighteen, at the height of her fame and beauty.

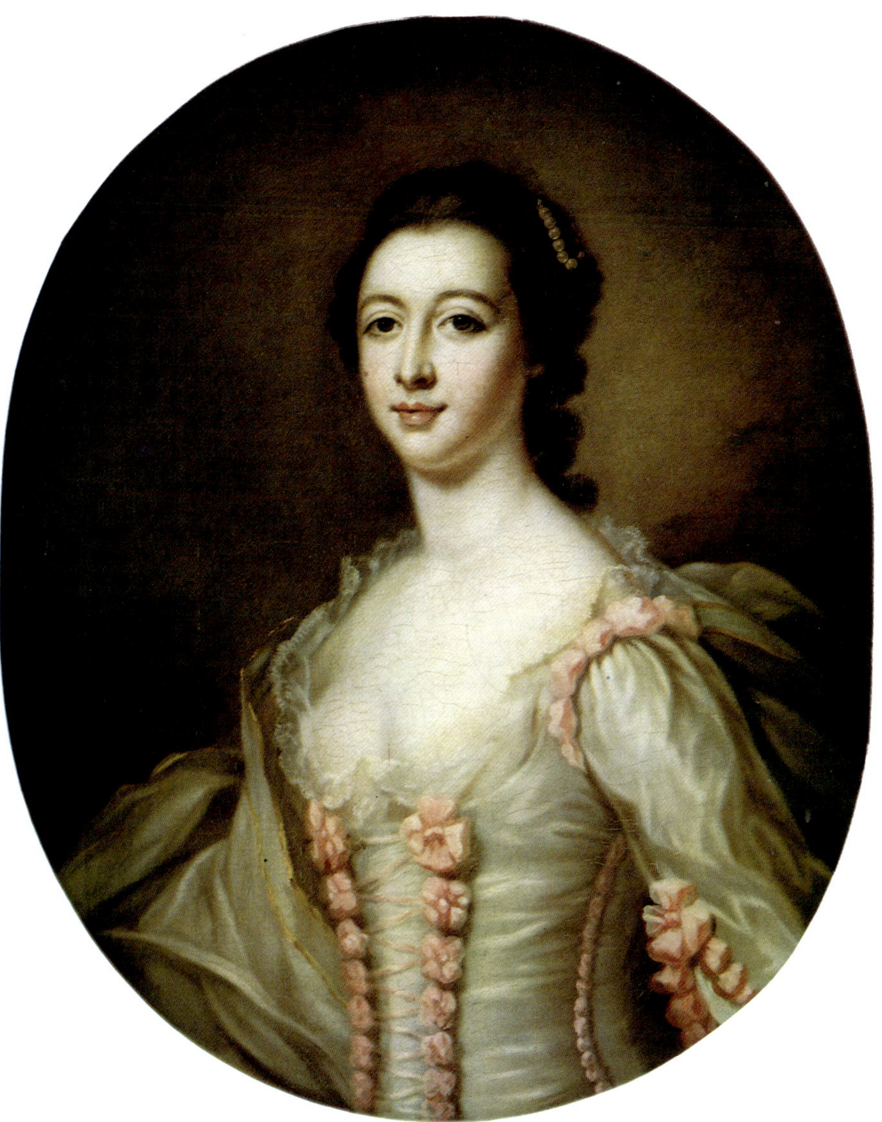

Francis Cotes, 1726-1770
Portrait of **MARIA GUNNING, COUNTESS OF COVENTRY,**
1733-1760, Beauty
Oil on canvas, 75 x 62 cms. Purchased, 1894

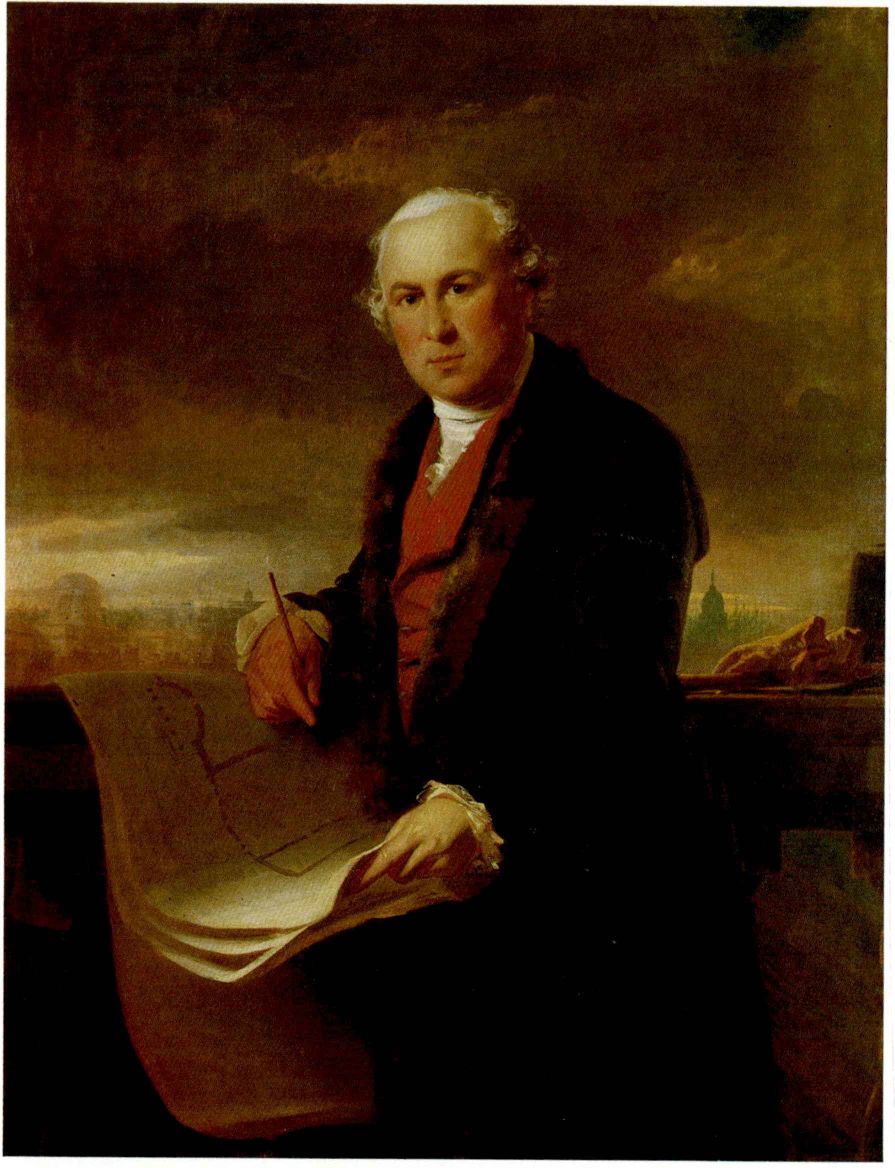

Tilly Kettle, 1735-1786 and *William Cuming* 1769-1852
Portrait of **JAMES GANDON,** 1743-1823. Architect
Oil on canvas, 123 x 98 cms. Purchased, 1965

James Gandon was the architect of many of the finest public buildings of Georgian Dublin. He studied architecture in his native London with one of the foremost architects of the day, Sir William Chambers. He soon set up his own practice and submitted designs for some of the buildings then being contemplated for Dublin by the Wide Streets Commission. He came to Dublin in 1781 to supervise the construction of the new Custom House. He remained in Ireland for much of his life, and designed, as well as the Custom House, the Four Courts and King's Inn, and also the portico of the House of Lords in College Green. Work did not always proceed without controversy and Gandon resigned in frustration from his work on the Four Courts before it was completed. He retired to spend his last years in a house he designed for himself near Lucan.

This portrait shows Gandon standing on the roof of the Parliament House with a view of the city quays behind him, compressed with artistic licence to show several of his most famous buildings. A mile long stretch of the Liffey is seen including the Four Courts, the Rotunda and the Custom House, and in his hands Gandon holds his plans for the Custom House.

Two artists were involved with this painting. Tilly Kettle was an English portrait painter, fleeing from his creditors, who came to Dublin for a few years en route to India. He had completed only the head before departing and it was left to another friend of Gandon's to complete the work. William Cuming, an Irish miniature and portrait painter, added the rest of the figure and the cityscape in the background. There was some delay before the painting was finished as Gandon's plans for the Custom House were not completed until several years after Kettle's departure.

Mary Tighe was the child of a Dublin clergyman, the Rev. William Blachford, Librarian for a time of Marsh's Library. Her mother was an active founder-member of the Methodist Movement in Ireland. Mary married her cousin, Henry Tighe of Woodstock, County Wicklow, a member of Parliament until the Union. The marriage was not a happy one, however, and Mary immersed herself in literature. She wrote a lengthy poem called *Psyche or the Legend of Love,* which was privately published in 1805. Her family did not altogether approve of this unladylike activity, but the poem was a resounding success and went into many editions. Thomas Moore (q.v.) much admired the poem, but felt success had turned Mrs. Tighe into an intellectual, 'One used hardly to get a peep at her blue stockings', he wrote, 'but now I am afraid she shows them up to her knee.'

The Romney portrait was painted in 1805, the year *Psyche* was published, and already signs of the consumption which was to kill her were evident. Of the portrait, Mary Tighe wrote to her family, 'It is pretty, but perfectly pallid among the high-coloured Lady Hamiltons and Mrs. Tickells . . . I wonder how it came to be so pale. I suppose everyone goes rouged to be painted. Bess's (her sister-in-law) picture is more generally approved, I think; mine looks as if a pretty woman had wept herself pale and sick'.

George Romney was a popular portrait painter at this time in England, although not as great an artist as his contemporaries Reynolds and Gainsborough. He was closely connected with Lady Hamilton and painted many portraits of her in classical pose. His portrait of Mary Tighe was later copied for use as a frontispiece for several editions of *Psyche.*

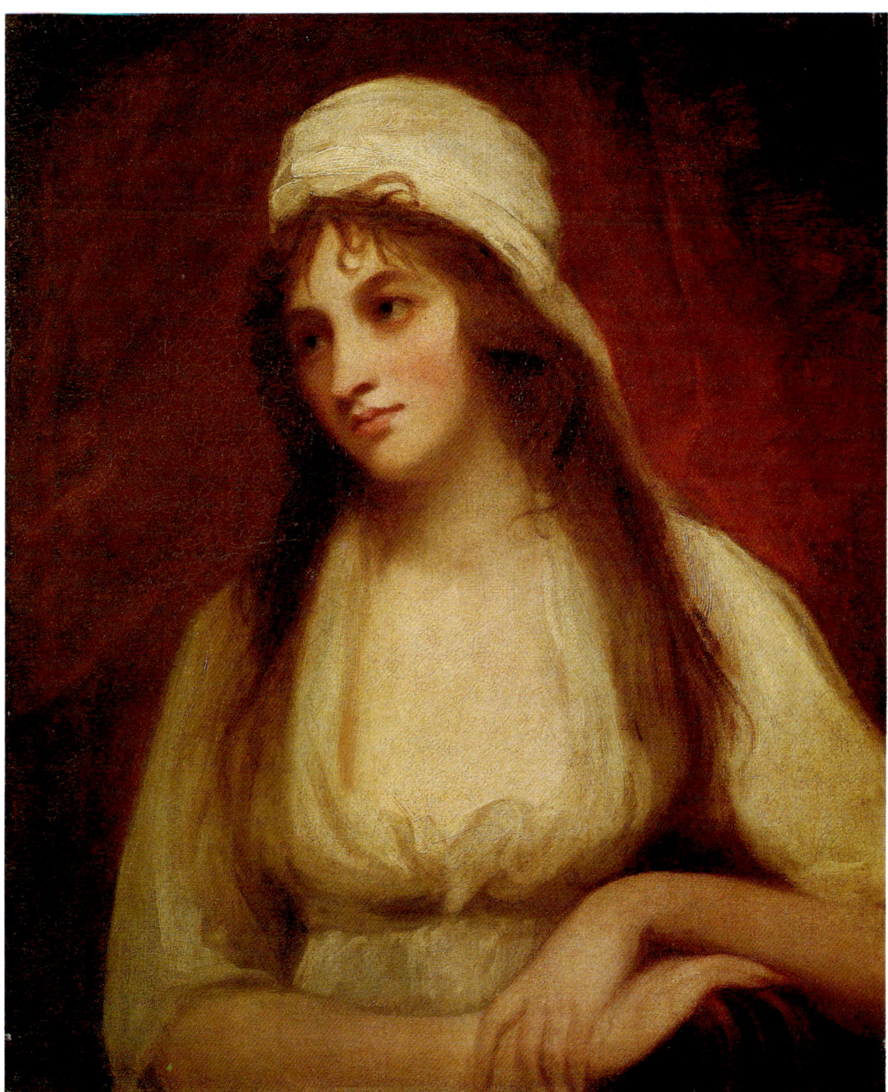

George Romney, 1734-1802
Portrait of **MARY TIGHE,** 1770/2-1810, Poet
Oil on canvas, 77 x 63 cms. Purchased, 1948

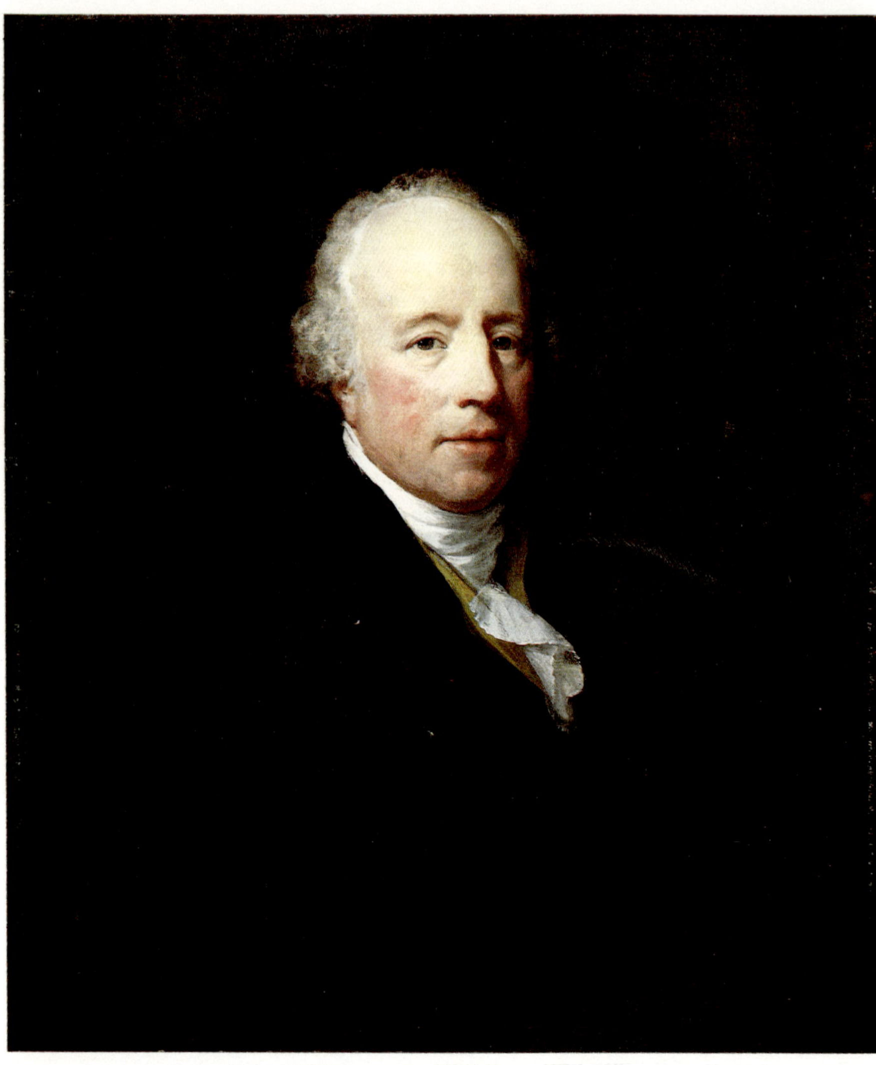

Hugh Douglas Hamilton, 1740-1808
Portrait of **RICHARD LOVELL EDGEWORTH,** 1744-1817,
Author and Inventor
Oil on canvas, 77 x 65 cms. Presented by Mrs. R. Montagu, 1956

Born into a family that gave its name to Edgeworthstown, County Longford, Richard Lovell Edgeworth showed an early precocity for science and throughout his life a stream of inventions and ideas flowed from his fertile mind. While still a student he designed a telegraphic contraption to help friends place winning bets at Newmarket. Later, when he settled on the family estate at Edgeworthstown, his inventions became more practical and he devised schemes for draining bogs, surfacing roads — with a process later developed by Macadam — and well in advance of his time, he invented caterpillar wheels, a pedometer or land measuring machine based on horse power, and even an automated turnip cutter.

Edgeworth's educational ideas were equally interesting. He advocated national and vocational education for both sexes of all classes. His eldest son was raised on the principles of Rousseau, and he supported his friend Thomas Day's attempt to educate an orphan girl to become the perfect wife, neither project meeting with much success. Edgeworth's daughter Maria, the celebrated writer, was his co-author on several books on agriculture and education, and he much encouraged her writings. Her first stories were written as educational tales for her eighteen brothers and sisters.

Hamilton studied under West at the Dublin Society Schools and became a successful portrait painter in pastel. While living in Italy he turned to oil and on his return to Dublin painted many portraits in this medium. The Edgeworth portrait was completed by 1800 and shows the artist's liking for chiaroscuro effects in his later works.

Richard Brinsley Sheridan was undoubtedly the most famous member of that most gifted literary family, the Sheridans. Born in Dublin, he spent many of his early years in Bath where his father ran a school. There he met and eloped with his first wife, the beautiful Elizabeth Linley, known as the Maid of Bath, in a romantic bid to save her from an arranged marriage. A flight to France, two duels, and sundry other adventures finally terminated in marriage and the story, loosely applied, became the plot of Sheridan's first play *The Rivals*.

Early success as a playwright provided Sheridan with the means to purchase the Drury Lane Theatre from Garrick and thereafter he played an important role in the theatrical life of London. Apart from his successful career as a dramatist he became interested in politics and entered Parliament to work with Charles James Fox, holding office under the brief Whig Governments. A confidant of the Prince of Wales, he supported the movement for a Regency. His high lifestyle and extravagant ways led him into debt and when the Drury Lane Theatre burned down in 1809 he had to be rescued from debtors prison by a public subscription. A lavish funeral demonstrated the affections in which he was held by the public when he was buried in Westminster Abbey.

Thomas Kirk was a Cork born artist and in 1808 was commissioned to execute the statue of Nelson which once adorned the centre of O'Connell Street, Dublin. He was subsequently commissioned to do many other public monuments, but he was also successful as a portrait sculptor, his busts being considered accurate representations of the sitters. A founder member of the Royal Hibernian Academy, Kirk was a prolific exhibitor at the annual exhibitions until his death.

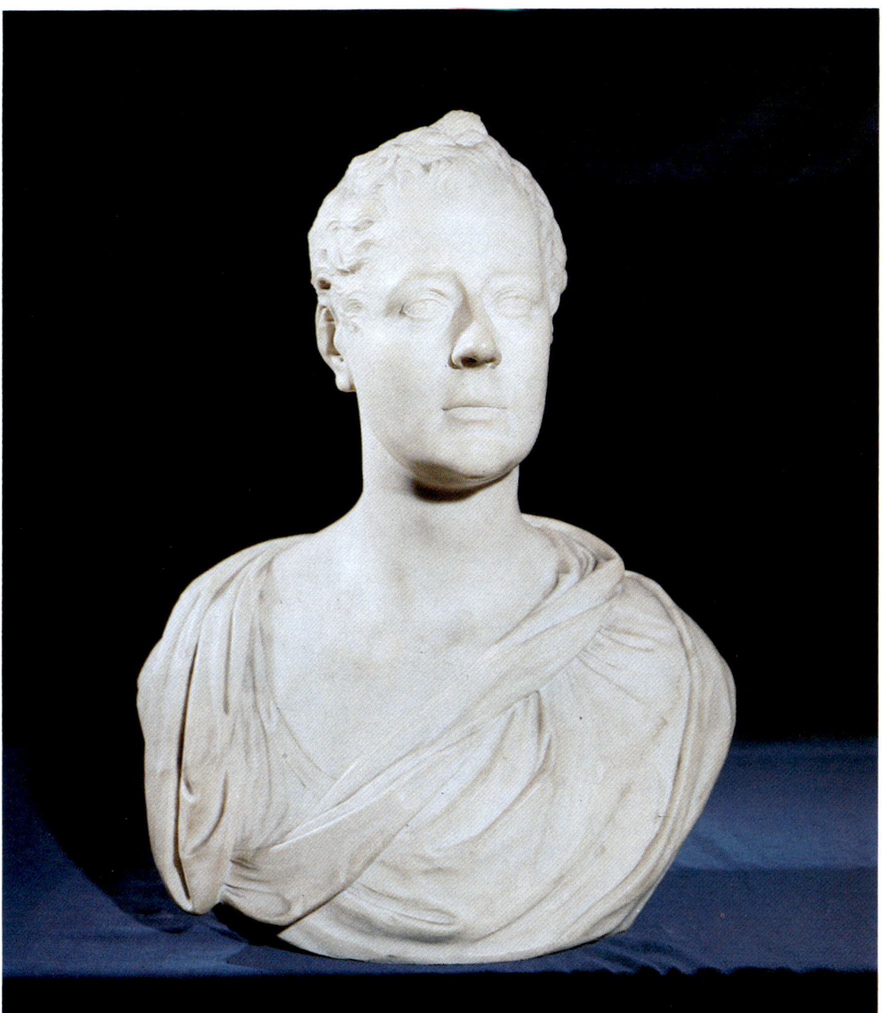

Thomas Kirk, 1781-1845
Portrait of **RICHARD BRINSLEY SHERIDAN,** 1751-1816, Dramatist and Politician.
Signed and dated: *Thos. Kirk, R.H.A., Fecit 1824*. Marble, Ht. 0.72 cms.
Purchased, 1943

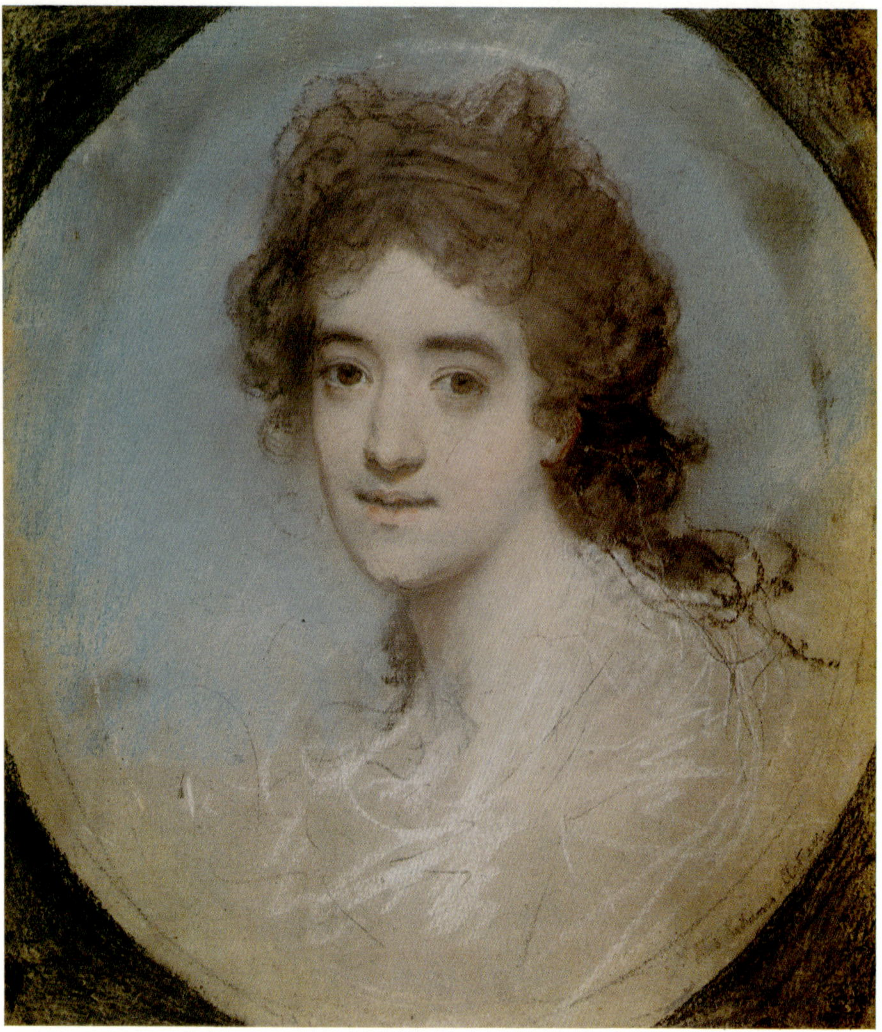

Ozias Humphry, 1742-1810
Portrait of **ELIZABETH FARREN,** later Countess of Derby, d.1829,
Actress
Pastel on paper, 23.6 x 20.9 cms. Purchased, 1889

Elizabeth Farren was born into a theatrical family in Cork. When her father drank himself to death, Elizabeth became a child actress and toured the English provinces for many years before making her first appearance in London at the age of eighteen. She was well received and for twenty years played leading roles at Drury Lane. Walpole considered her the best actress he had ever seen and named her Queen of Comedy. Charles Fox admired her greatly until he saw her wearing breeches on stage, and in 1797 she gave a tearful last performance as Lady Teazle and retired from the stage to marry another long time admirer, Edward Stanley, 12th Earl of Derby.

Despite her humble origins and close assocations with Fox and the Earl of Derby, Eliza Farren's career seems to have been more notable for its extreme virtue than for any great acting ability. She was much admired for her portrayal of 'fine ladies' and was praised for the innate delicacy with which she 'slurred many a risky passage in the old dramatists'. After her marriage she was received at court and became a great favourite of Queen Caroline.

Ozias Humphry was one of the finest English miniaturists of his day, famed for his elegant portraits. Failing eyesight eventually forced him to abandon miniatures for crayon drawings and this portrait was one of his last works, exhibited at the Royal Academy in 1794. An earlier miniature of the actress by Humphry elicited a long and rather bad poem from the Earl of Derby.

'. . . Pleas'd, I behold the fair whose
    comic art
Th'unwearied eye of taste and
    Judgement draws,
Who charms with nature's elegance
    the heart . . .'

A most unwilling Irishman, Arthur Wellesley, Duke of Wellington, once responded to being called Irish with his famous remark, 'Because a man is born in a stable, that does not make him a horse.' Born at Mornington House in Dublin, he was a younger son of the Earl of Mornington. He served as Aide-de-Camp to the Lord Lieutenant of Ireland and became M.P. for Trim before being sent to India with his regiment. He led several successful campaigns in India, was knighted in 1804 and recalled to Europe where the Napoleonic wars were now raging. In 1809 he was given command of the Penninsular army and successfully drove the French from Spain. After Napoleon's defeat, Wellesley was made Duke of Wellington and granted £400,000 by a grateful Parliament. When Napoleon escaped from Elba, Wellington was given command of all the British forces and led them to victory at the Battle of Waterloo. This was the notable end to his military career. He later joined the Cabinet and was for many years a notoriously reactionary politican who opposed Parliamentary reform.

Despite his disinterest in his native country, as Chief Secretary for Ireland, Wellington reformed the Dublin police and laid the foundations of the Irish Constabulary. He was much occupied with the Irish Question, and during his brief period as Prime Minister he was responsible for passing the Bill for Catholic Emancipation — much against his will.

John Lucas was an English artist who made a successful career as a portrait painter. He painted many portraits of the 'Iron Duke', who approved of his portraits, and here he shows Wellington in the uniform of Field Marshal with his cloak thrown open to reveal the ribbon of the Garter.

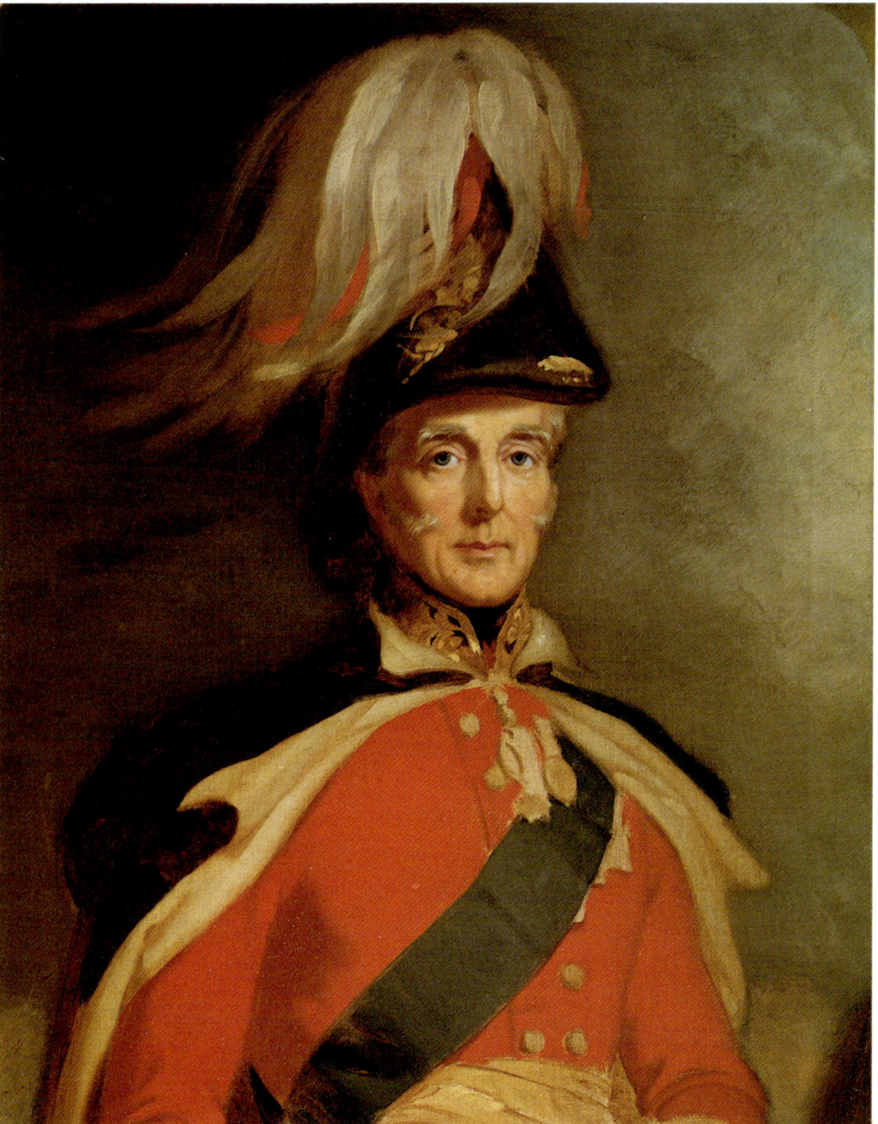

John Lucas, 1807-1874
Portrait of **ARTHUR WELLESLEY,** 1st Duke of Wellington, 1769-1852, Soldier
Oil on canvas, 97 x 74 cms. Purchased, 1875

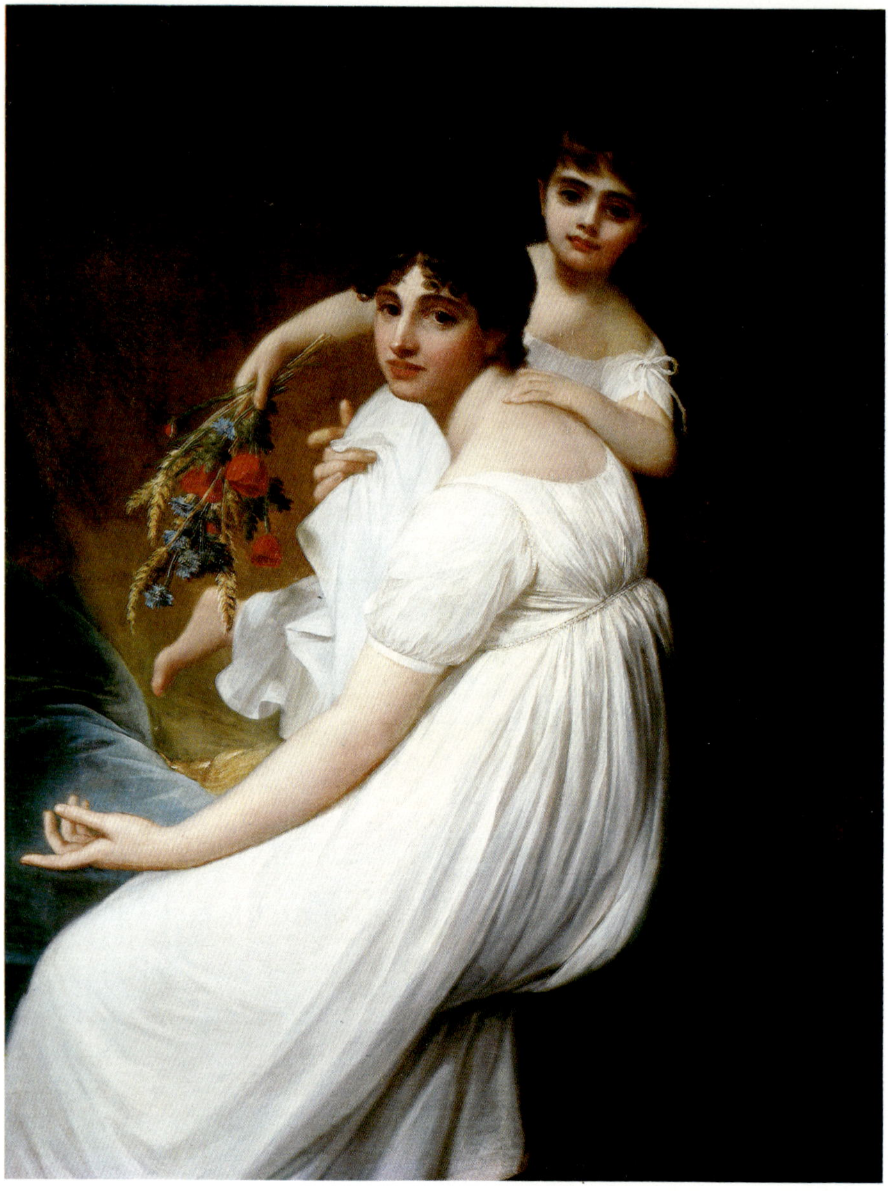

The beautiful Lady Pamela, wife of Lord Edward Fitzgerald, who flitted briefly into Irish history and departed as mysteriously, was painted with her daughter, also called Pamela, in 1800. Lord Edward first caught sight of his future wife at the Paris Opera and, smitten with love, married her at once despite the mystery surrounding her birth. Probably born in the West Indies, Pamela was adopted by Mme. de Genlis to be a companion to her charges, the children of the Duc d'Orléans. Rumours circulated that the beautiful girl was a love child of the Duke and the famous writer.

Pamela was not concerned with such matters, however, and lived happily at Frascati House, near Dublin, indulging in her passion for dancing and with no thought for her husband's increasing involvement in politics. Their third child was born while Lord Edward was in hiding, and after his death Lady Pamela was ordered out of the country and his lands were confiscated. Little is known of her later life. With Europe in turmoil, she moved from city to city, and an unhappy second marriage did not last long. Pamela ended her days in poverty and obscurity, dying in Paris at the age of 57.

This painting was owned by the family of Pamela's youngest child until presented to the Gallery. Despite the beauty of the work, nothing is known of the artist, apart from a letter referring to him as a French emigré who painted Pamela in Hamburg.

Mallary (fl. c.1800)
Portrait of **LADY PAMELA FITZGERALD,** d.1831. With her Daughter
Oil on canvas, 130 x 100 cms. Presented by Mrs. P. Selby-Smith, 1976

Robert Emmet was born in Dublin where his father was physician to the Viceroy. He distinguished himself at Trinity College as an orator in the Historical Society, and like his older brother Thomas Addis Emmet, he became a leader of the United Irishmen. Because of this political activity he was expelled from the College after the Rebellion of 1798 and for a time joined his brother in exile in Paris. He tried, without success, to interest Napoleon in supporting another rebellion and returned to Dublin to reorganise the United Irishmen.

During the Rising of 1803 Emmet led a disorganised band of his followers to storm Dublin Castle. Instead, they attacked the carriage of Lord Kilwarden, the Chief Justice, and killed him and his nephew. Emmet fled to the Dublin mountains but was arrested as he tried to meet his fiancée, Sarah Curran, daughter of John Philpot Curran. He was tried, found guilty of treason and hanged in Thomas Street, Dublin on 20th September 1803. His famous speech from the dock is still quoted on emotive political occassions and his love for Sarah Curran is remembered in Moore's ballads: *Speak not his Name* and *She is far from the land*.

John Comerford was a Kilkenny artist who settled in Dublin about 1800. He was a successful miniaturist and a self-taught artist. He opposed the founding of the Royal Hibernian Academy as he feared it would encourage mediocre artists. This fine example of his work was presented to the Irish Nation by the Emmet family and according to family tradition, it was sketched by Comerford during Emmet's trial.

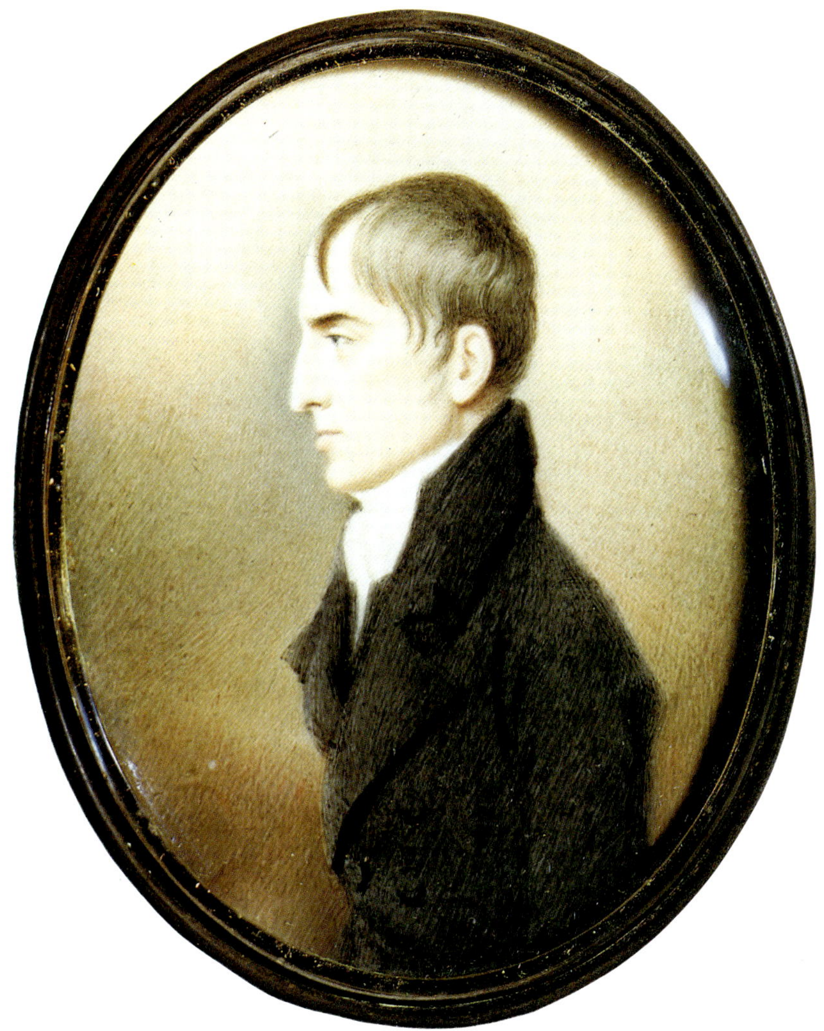

John Comerford, ?1770-1832
Portrait of **ROBERT EMMET,** 1778-1803, Patriot
Watercolour on ivory, 6.9 x 5.7 cms. Presented by Mr. R. Emmet to the Irish Government, 1969. Transferred to the National Gallery 1970

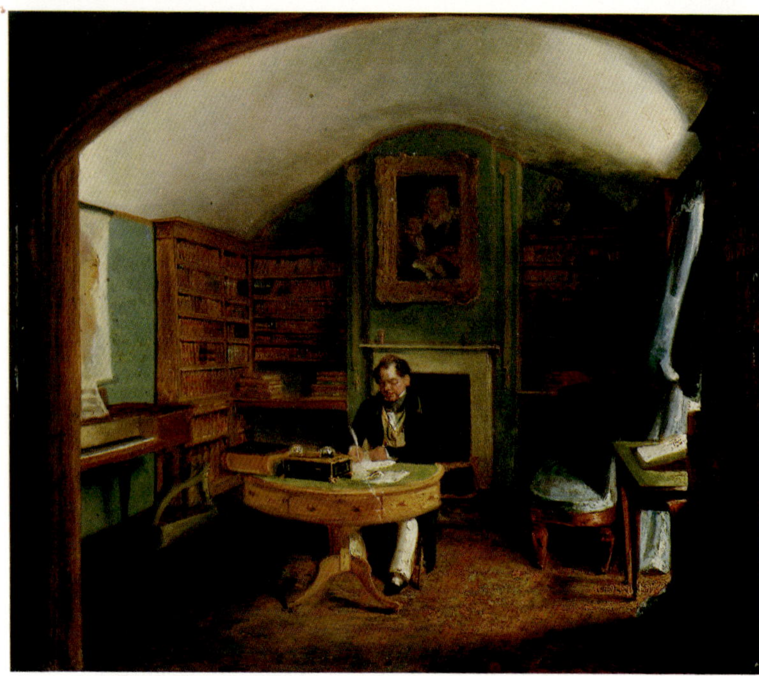

English School 19th Century
Portrait of **THOMAS MOORE**, 1779-1852, Poet
In his study at Sloperton Cottage
Oil on panel, 30 x 36 cms. Purchased, 1978

Thomas Moore was born in Aungier Street, Dublin, where his birth-place still stands. Born into a Catholic family, he entered Trinity College to study law soon after the anti-Catholic laws prohibiting this were repealed. He began to write verse as a child and his first novel was published under the thinly disguised pseudonym of Thomas Little. With no private income of his own, Moore was dependant on writing for his living and was soon publishing poetry and biographies. *Lalla Rookh* earned him the greatest sum ever paid for a poem to that date. In 1807 he embarked on his most successful venture, the writing of suitable verse for old Irish tunes, which was to occupy him for the next twenty-five years. These were published in a series of ten volumes of *Irish Melodies,* and firmly established him as a popular poet. He often performed these songs in public, accompanying himself on the piano or harp.

Moore's pleasant personality and easy manner won him friends everywhere throughout his life. He was a close friend of Byron who entrusted him with the manuscript of his *Memoirs* on condition that they were not published during the author's lifetime. After Byron's death Lady Byron protested at their publication and Moore gallantly bought them back from the publisher and burned them. He later made some attempt to rectify matters by writing Byron's life himself, and editing his letters.

This unusual portrait of the poet shows him working in his study at Sloperton Cottage, Wiltshire, where he spent his later years. The writing well on the table belonged to Crabbe and inspired Moore to write his *Lines to Crabbe's inkstand.* Moore's widow later gave this inkstand to Mrs. S.C. Hall (q.v.), who in her *Memoir of Thomas Moore* described the room as it appears here, even down to the Irish harp which 'occasionally accompanied him to friendly parties'.

24

The early years of Lady Sydney Morgan might have been taken from the pages of one of her own novels. She is generally thought to have been born about 1783, although she herself remained vague on the subject. She grew up in the raffish world of the Theatre Royal, Dublin, where her father was actor-manager. She worked briefly as a governess until she published a small volume of her own verse set to Irish tunes, in the manner later popularized by Thomas Moore (q.v.). Inspired by the financial success of Fanny Burney she embarked on novel writing and her *Wild Irish Girl* was an immediate triumph and paved the way for later popular romantic novels.

At her house in Kildare Street, Dublin, Lady Morgan held a literary salon at which sooner or later everyone of social or literary note in Dublin was found. She travelled widely and used her experiences of continental life in her novels, but it was her depictions of Irish life that were most successful. Her sympathies with the Irish peasant and the strong nationalistic sentiments as expressed in her writings made her a popular figure with Catholic Emancip-ationists and Liberals. She was the first woman to receive a pension for writing.

While on a trip to Italy, Lady Morgan paused in Paris to have her portrait painted by René Théodore Berthon, then considered to be one of David's best pupils, and a painter of portraits and historical subjects. 'It is', she wrote to a friend, 'to be as large as life, no very immoderate dimension that! . . . Kildare Street, be proud!' The painting, which hung in her boudoir in Kildare Street, was engraved as a frontispiece to her *Passages from my Autobiography,* and was bequeathed by her to the Irish Nation.

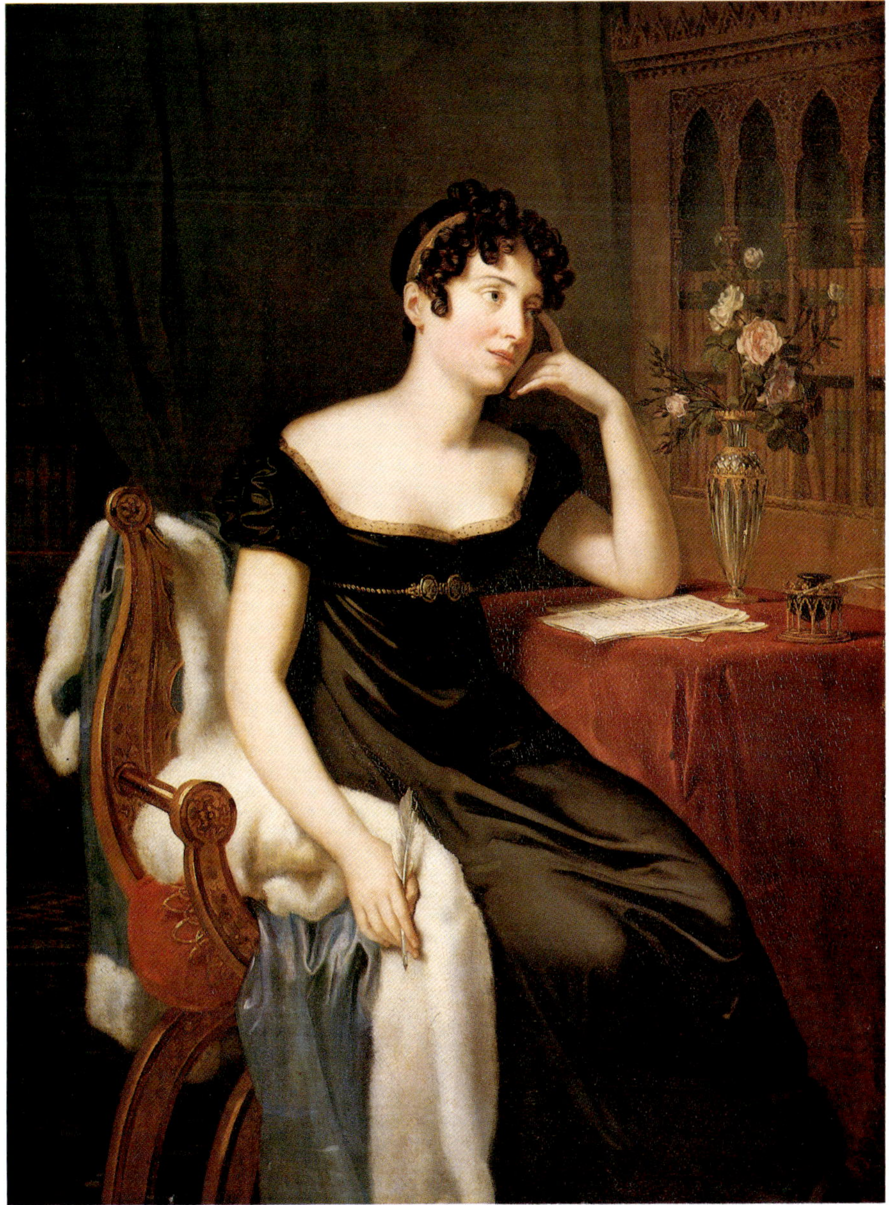

René Berthon, 1776-1859
Portrait of **LADY MORGAN,** c.1783-1859. Writer. Signed: *Berthon*
Oil on canvas, 130 x 98 cms. c.1783. Lady Morgan Bequest, 1860

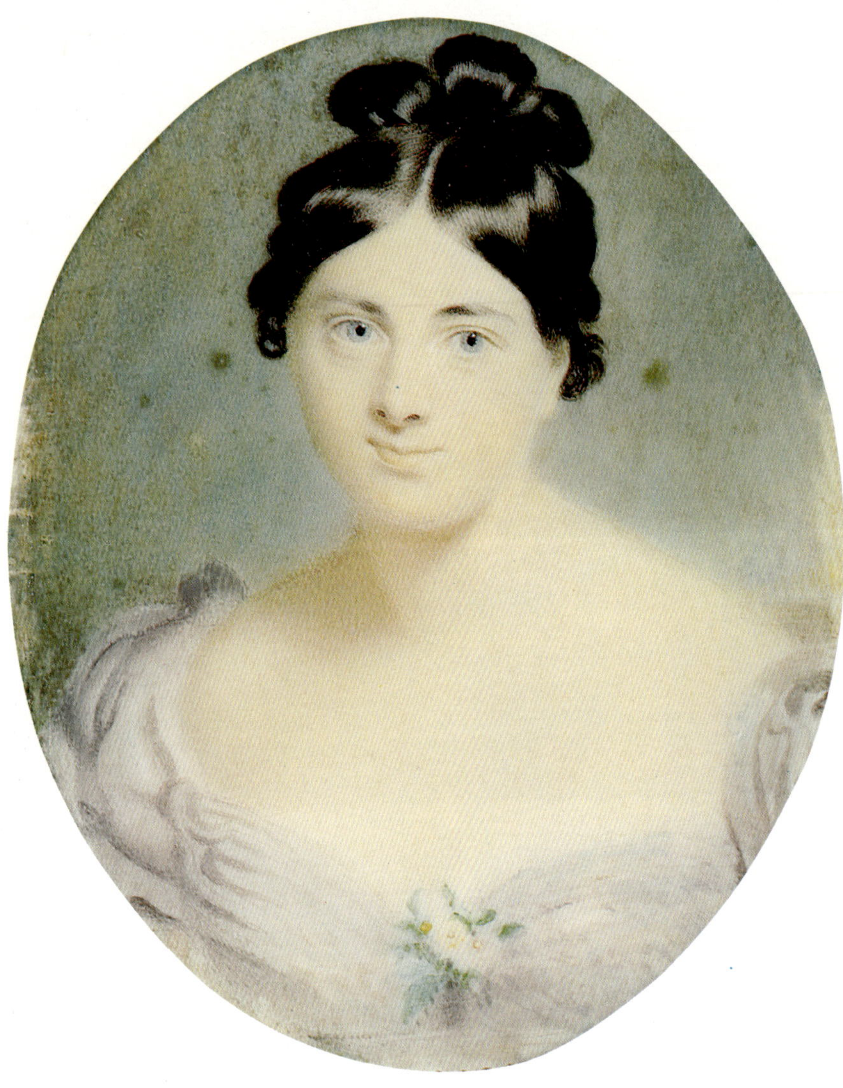

After *T. Lawrence* 1769-1830
Portrait of **MARGUERITE POWER,** Countess of Blessington, 1789-1849,
Writer
Watercolour on ivory, 7.5 x 7.8 cms. Purchased, 1890

Marguerite, Countess of Blessington, probably inherited her talent for writing from her father, Edward Power, who was sometime editor of the *Clonmel Gazette* and *Munster Mercury*. She grew up in Clonmel, County Tipperary and there at the age of 14 was forced into marriage with a dissolute army officer. She ran away from him to London where she was soon noticed for her beauty. When her husband died in a prison brawl some years later she married the widowed 1st Earl of Blessington. They spent the next few years travelling extravagantly on the Continent, living and entertaining in the grand manner. In their entourage was the Count d'Orsay, an amateur artist and dandy, considered to be the handsomest man of his time. When the Earl died suddenly of apoplexy in Paris, Lady Blessington returned to live in London, accompanied by the Count.

For twenty years Lady Blessington held a salon at her house in Kensington where she received all the literary and social notables of her day. She produced a series of light romantic novels which had great vogue as well as contributing social notes, or in today's terms, a gossip column, to the *Daily Mail*. Despite her considerable earnings and a pension from her husband's estate, Lady Blessington's extravagant lifestyle still led her into debt. In 1849 the Count d'Orsay slipped quietly out of London, followed a few days later by Lady Blessington in an attempt to escape her creditors. She died a few months later in Paris.

This miniature of Lady Blessington is one of several taken from an oil painting by Sir Thomas Lawrence, which is now in the Wallace Collection, London. The painting shows her at the age of eighteen, when she was already considered a great beauty.

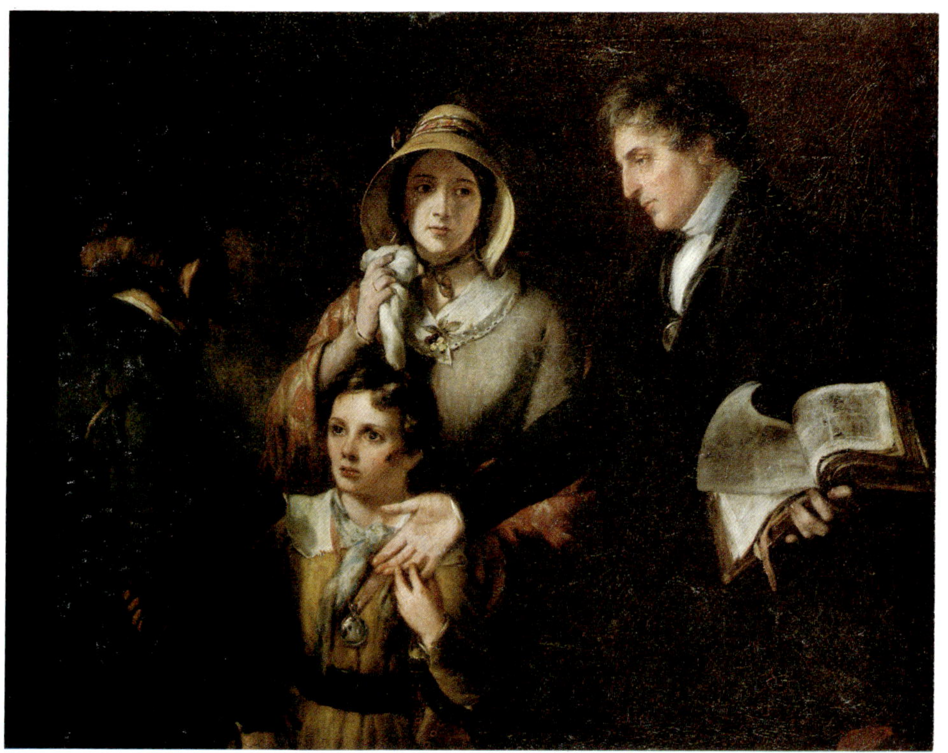

Joseph Haverty, 1794-1864
Portrait of **FATHER THEOBALD MATHEW,** 1790-1856,
Apostle of Temperance, receiving a Repentant Pledge-Breaker
Oil on canvas, 107 x 137 cms. Purchased, 1971

Father Theobald Mathew, the Apostle of Temperance, entered the Capuchin order in Dublin as a young man. For many years his ministry was in the poorest areas of Cork city where he founded free schools for the young and a society for the distribution of alms. In 1835 friends invited him to head the newly formed Temperance Movement, and with the words 'Here goes, in the name of the Lord' he signed the pledge and began his life's mission.

Father Mathew's temperance campaign was an outstanding success from the beginning. Crowds flocked to hear him preach against the evils of drink and stayed to take the pledge. Half the adult Irish population became teetotal within a few years. Government revenue from duty on spirits fell from £1.4 million to £0.8 million and crime dwindled to almost nothing. He was invited to tour Irish centres in Britain, and to visit the United States where he was received in the House of Representatives and talked with the President. The Vatican finally offered to make him a Bishop, but overwork had taken its toll and ill health forced him to refuse the honour. His final years were spent in Cobh, County Cork, where he lived with his brother's family.

Haverty was a Galway artist, and seems to have worked there and in Limerick for most of his life. He was a successful portrait and genre painter, but it was his efforts to record important events in Irish life for which he is best remembered. This painting shows Father Mathew saving a repentant sinner from the evils of drink and demonstrates Haverty's ability to draw sympathy from his audience.

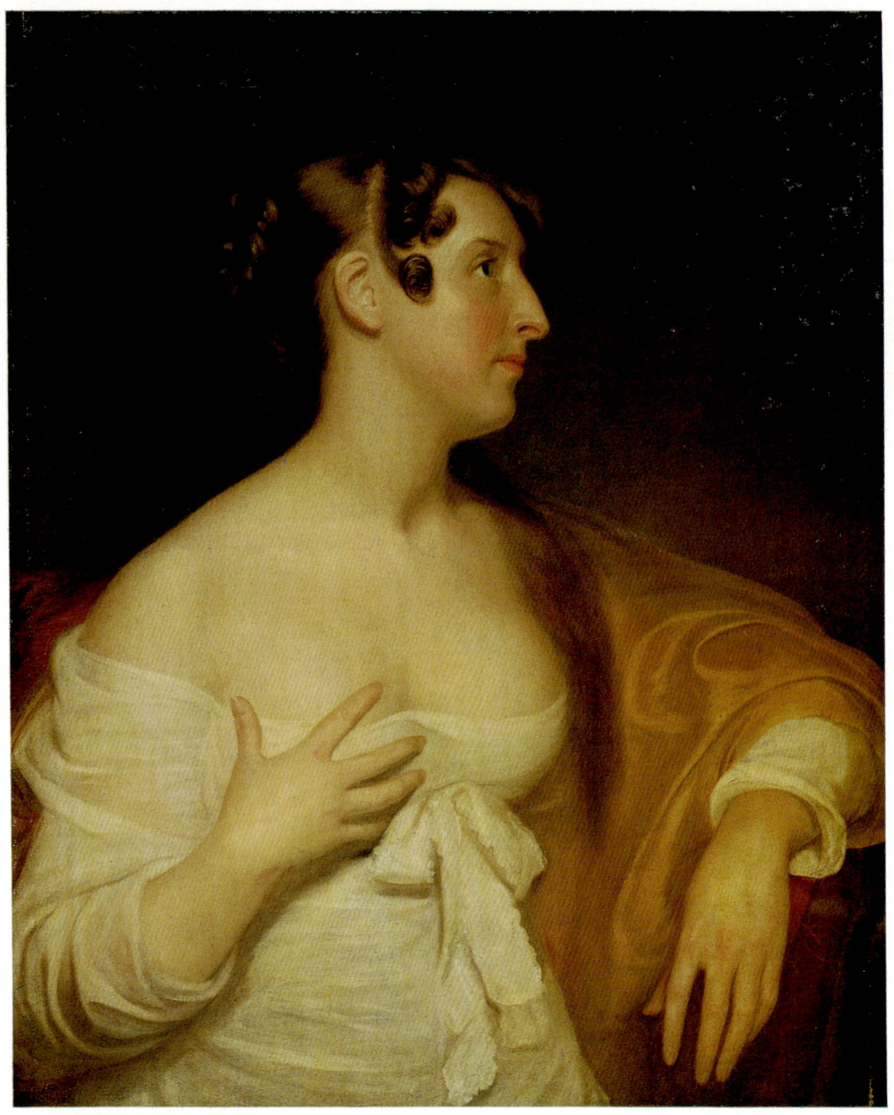

Thomas Clement Thompson, c. 1780-1857.
Portrait of **ELIZA O'NEILL**, 1791-1872, Actress
Oil on canvas, 59 x 50 cms. Purchased, 1910

Eliza O'Neill was born in Drogheda, County Louth where her father was actor manager of the local theatre. She made her first appearance on the stage as a child and was soon playing children's parts with success in Dublin and Belfast. She was 'discovered' by a London impresario who was sufficiently impressed by her performance to agree to a succession of poor Irish relatives accompanying her to London as part of her contract. Eliza O'Neill made her London debut as Juliet at Covent Garden in 1814. Her success was immediate and for several years she was in great demand for the major tragic roles. Her brief but meteoric career ended with her marriage to an Irish squire, William Becher.

Eliza O'Neill's career lasted only five years but her performances were remembered long after her retirement. She was admired for her classic beauty and grecian profile, and for her voice and carriage. She was compared with Mrs. Siddons and described as the last great tragic actress. Such was the effect of her performances that grown men were carried fainting from the theatre. She had a reputation for avarice, possibly because of having to support numerous indigent relatives, and Thackeray's most unflattering portrayal of her as Miss Fotheringay in *Pendennis* cruelly emphasises this trait as well as her Irish brogue. The caricature can only have been based on hearsay, however, since she retired from the stage when Thackeray was a child.

Thomas Clement Thompson was trained at the Dublin Society Schools and worked as a miniature artist in Belfast and Dublin before turning to oil portraits. He moved to London and had a successful career as a portrait painter, continuing to exhibit at the Royal Academy and Royal Hibernian Academy exhibitions.

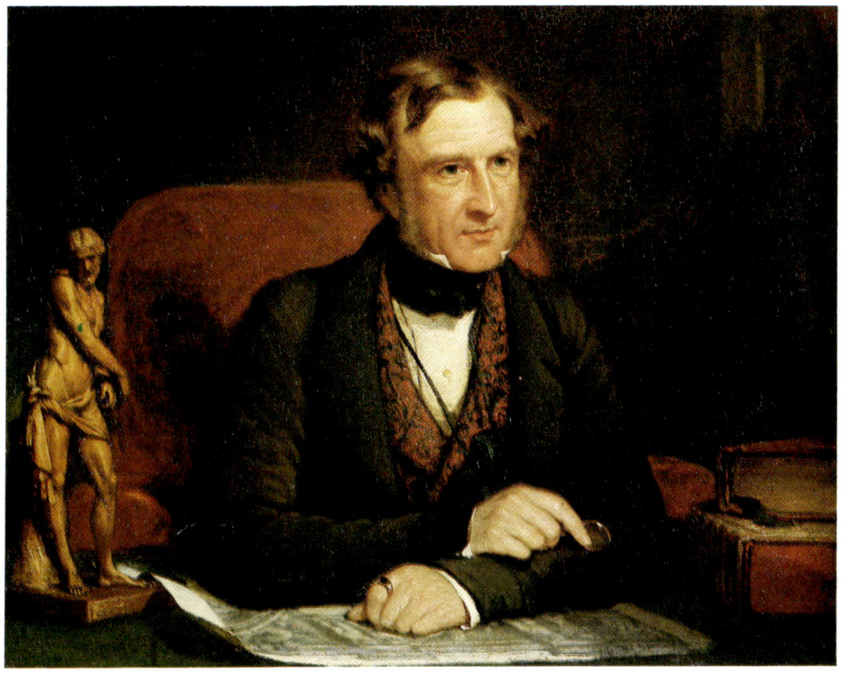

John Partridge, 1790-1872
Portrait of **THOMAS WYSE**, 1791-1862, Author, Parliamentarian and Diplomat
Oil on canvas, 71 x 91 cms. Purchased, 1874

Thomas Wyse was born into a Catholic landed family in County Waterford and attended the newly founded Catholic college of Stonyhurst with Richard Lalor Sheil and Nicholas Ball. While attending Trinity College Dublin he won medals for oratory and essays, and after this he spent four years on the Grand Tour, studying and sketching architecture in southern Europe and the Middle East. In Italy he married Laetitia, daughter of Lucien Bonaparte, but the marriage was not a success and they separated in 1828, leaving Wyse to raise their two children in Ireland.

Wyse returned to Ireland when agitation broke out over the question of Catholic Emancipation, and he entered politics, becoming M.P. for Tipperary and Waterford. He rivalled Sheil and O'Connell in importance on the Emancipation issue and, as an 'enlightened' Liberal, worked hard for popular education. He was instrumental in the passing of a bill to set up a Department of Education. He was appointed to the Fine Arts Commission for the Decoration of London's New Houses of Parliament, and Palmerston appointed him British Minister in Athens in 1849. He was highly regarded by the Greeks during his term of office and was given a state funeral in Athens when he died.

Partridge studied art in Italy and established himself as a fashionable portrait painter in London. He was a member of the Royal Academy but enemies within the Academy hung his works badly, and in protest he resigned. His career was badly affected by this and in an attempt to find independent patronage for himself, he painted a group portrait of the Commission for the Fine Arts of which Wyse was a member. The present portrait was a study for this work and shows Wyse with a sketch of the Houses of Parliament, and an antique statue representing his involvement in the arts.

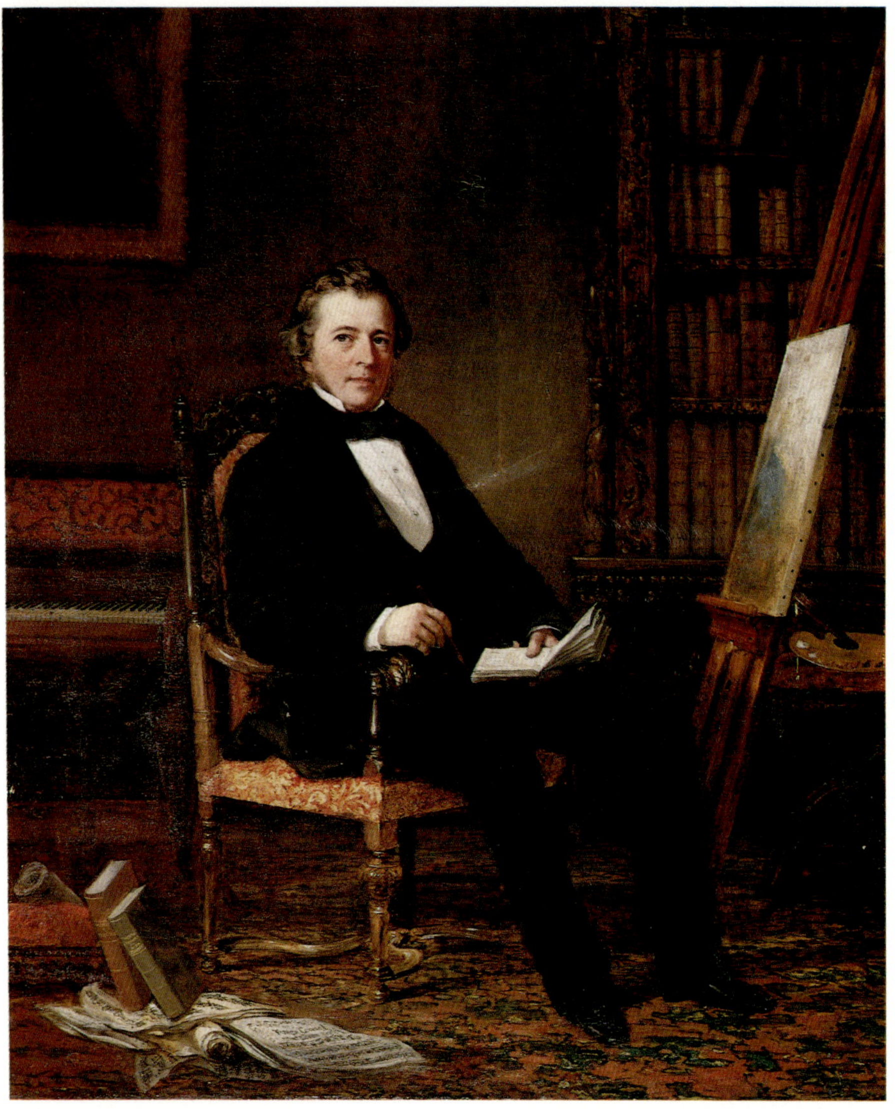

James Harwood, 1816-1872
Portrait of **SAMUEL LOVER,** 1797-1868, Author and Artist
Oil on canvas, 74 x 61 cms. Purchased, 1872

The unlikely son of a Dublin stockbroker, Samuel Lover showed a talent for art and music from childhood. When his father disinherited him for refusing to enter the family business, Lover had little difficulty in earning his living from painting miniatures and publishing his own songs and ballads. Through friendship with Thomas Moore (q.v.) he had access to the social and literary life of Dublin and when he moved to London, his many accomplishments found him the same success. He frequented Lady Blessington's (q.v.) receptions and was a friend of Charles Dickens and other literary figures.

Lover was competent in almost any medium in which he chose to work. His popular early ballad, *Rory O'More,* became in his hands a successful novel, and then a play in which the Irish comic actor Tyrone Power played the lead role in a successful run of one hundred nights at London's Adelphi Theatre. He illustrated many of his own books and published an opera *buffo* delightfully entitled *Il Paddy Whack in Italia* which Balfe staged at his English Opera Company. Failing eyesight eventually forced Lover to abandon painting as his chief source of income and he compiled a one man show from his own works, consisting of recitations, songs and stories, which he called *Irish Evenings* and with this he successfully toured England, the United States and Canada.

This portrait by the artist James Harwood amply demonstrates Lover's many accomplishments. He sits in his study surrounded by his own books, paintings and music. Harwood was a Clonmel artist who spent many years working in London and Bath. He painted this portrait of Lover in 1856 for a Clonmel patron, whose wife sold it to the Gallery after showing it at the Dublin Exhibition of 1872.

John Banim studied art at the Dublin Society Schools and was active in the movement to establish a Charter of Incorporation for Irish artists, which eventually led to the founding of the Royal Hibernian Academy. He taught art in his native Kilkenny for some years, but an unhappy love affair altered him greatly and he abandoned art and turned for solace to literature. He went to London and it was there that he first conceived the idea of writing a series of 'Irish' novels drawing on native life and stories, which would do for Ireland, he hoped, 'what the Waverly novels did for Scotland'.

John Banim approached his older brother Michael, who had remained in Kilkenny, to join him in this venture, and together they produced the series of O'Hara Brothers novels, twenty-three in all, of which John wrote ten and which earned him the title 'Scott of Ireland'. Despite the success of the books, however, both brothers struggled with poverty for most of their lives. John suffered from a spinal disease which slowly paralysed him and made writing difficult. He worked on to the end of his life, in pain and poverty, supported by his brother Michael, who was himself burdened with the failing family business in Kilkenny.

George Mulvany was an active member of the Royal Hibernian Academy, succeeding his father as Keeper, and was a friend of John Banim. His portrait of the writer was in his possession at the time of his death and was later purchased by the Gallery from his daughter. Michael Banim considered it an excellent likeness of his brother, painted a few years before his death. It was used for the frontispiece of Murray's *Life of Banim,* and was also the model for Hogan's bust of the writer.

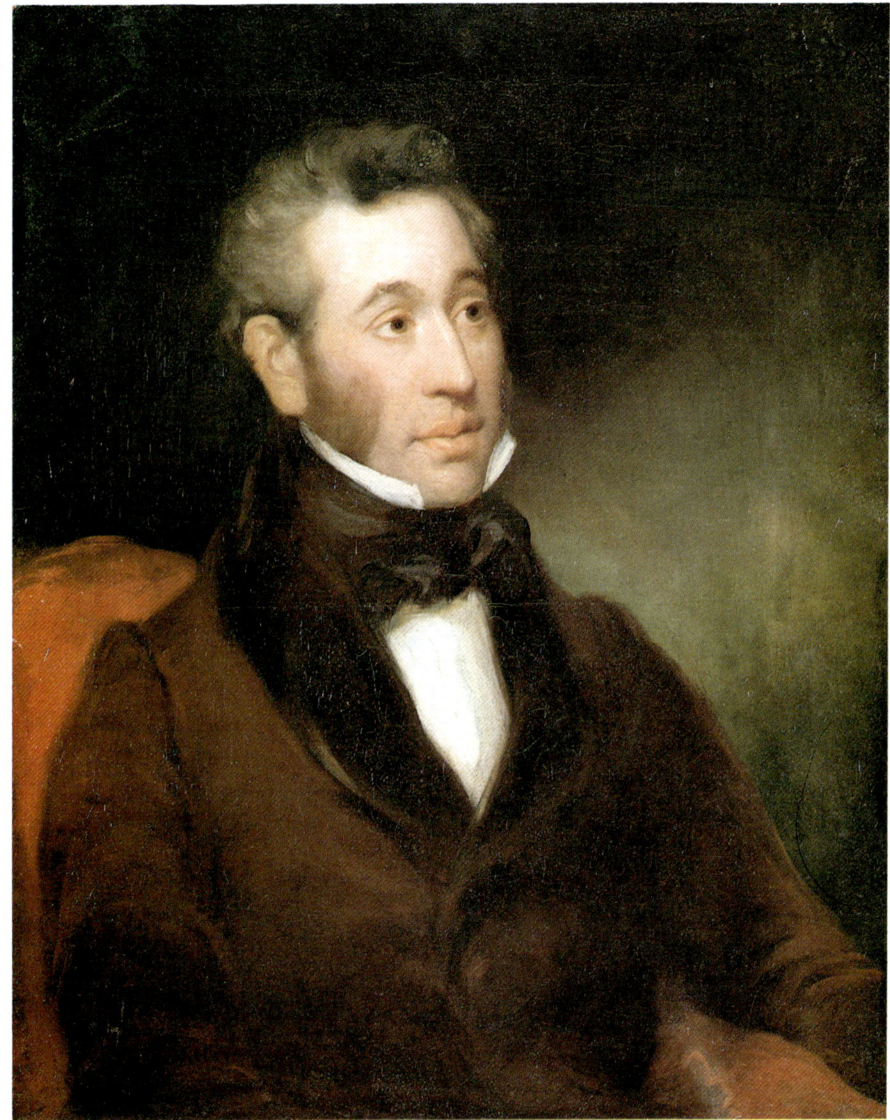

George Francis Mulvany, 1809-1869
Portrait of **JOHN BANIM,** 1798-1842, Novelist
Oil on canvas, 74 x 61 cms. Purchased, 1884

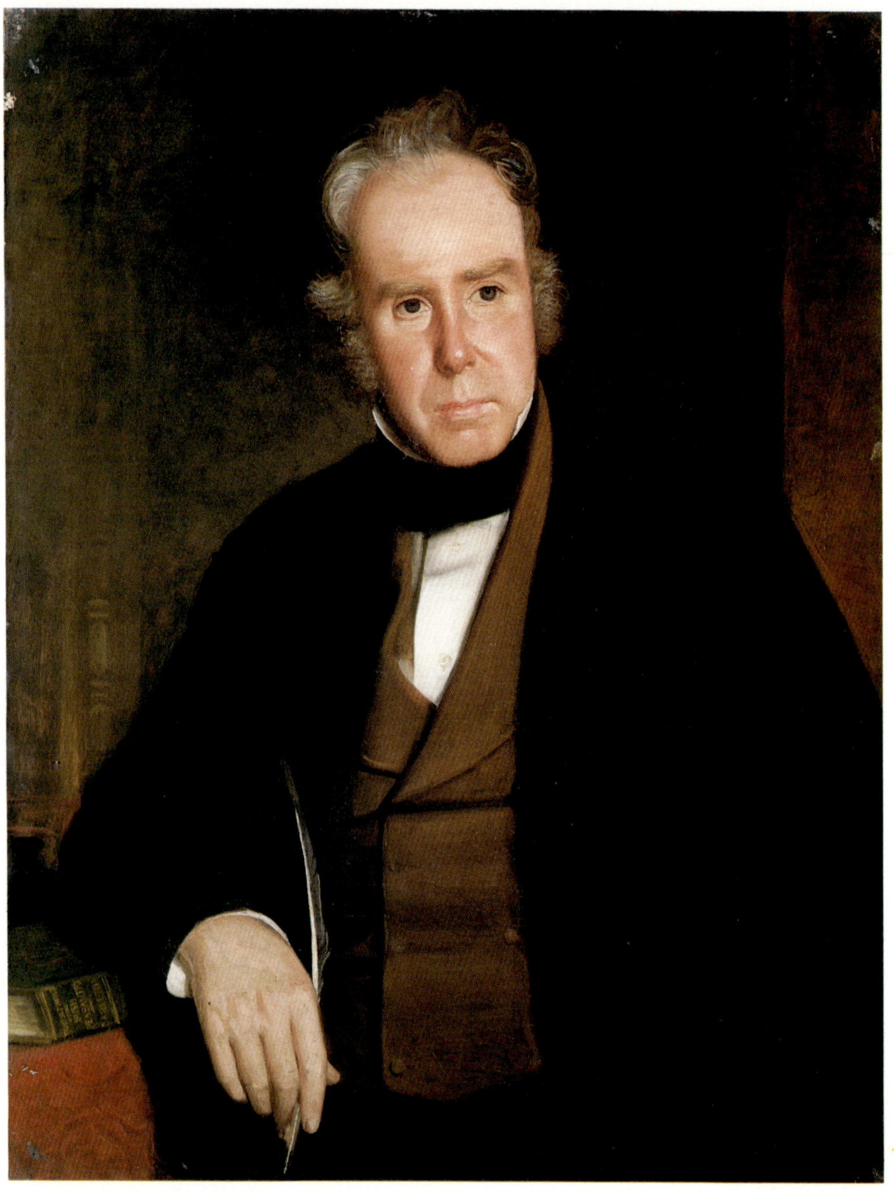

John Slattery, fl.1846-1858
Portrait of **WILLIAM CARLETON**, 1794-1869, Writer
Oil on canvas, 82 x 63 cms. Purchased, 1884

Born, according to his autobiography, in a peasant cottage at Prolusk, County Tyrone, William Carleton's early education was sketchy and harsh as he attended a succession of hedge schools in and about his native county. His family earmarked him for the priesthood but a pilgrimage to Lough Derg convinced him this was not the life for him. After an initial struggle to earn a living from tutoring, Carleton began to publish stories in newspapers and journals, and these were eventually published in one volume as *Traits and Stories of the Irish Peasantry*. He was a prolific writer, but like many Irish writers of his day could not support himself from his profession. Towards the end of his life a petition was addressed to the Government on his behalf, one of the signatories being Maria Edgeworth, and he was granted a state pension. His final years were devoted to an autobiography which was still unfinished at his death.

Carleton was conscious of his native origins and well situated to write of the Irish peasantry. His father was an accomplished storyteller, and his mother was a fund of traditional songs. Carleton himself was raised in a bilingual environment. He tried to represent the Irish peasant without the cariciature popular at the time, and many of his stories were semi-autobiographical. His tales provide an interesting insight into Irish country life in pre-famine times.

This painting was purchased from Carleton's daughter in 1884, some years after his death, and a letter from his widow says 'It is the only portrait of its kind ever taken of him, and is a most truthful one'. Slattery was a successful portrait painter working in Dublin until 1858, after which little is known about him but he may have emigrated to America.

Mrs. Samuel Carter Hall was born Anna Maria Fielding in Dublin in the year 1800. She moved to London where she met and married her husband, Samuel Carter Hall. He was already an established journalist and encouraged his wife to write 'just as you tell it,' and soon she was publishing a series of sketches of Irish life which were very successful and were collected into a volume entitled *Sketches of Irish Character*. She was a rapid and prolific writer and produced several volumes of stories, nine novels and some plays. She shared her husband's interest in spiritualism, and was involved with many charities including the Temperance Movement, for which she wrote pamphlets. She was a founder of the Brompton Hospital for Consumptives, the Governesses Institute, and the Home for Decayed Gentlewomen.

Throughout her life Mrs. Hall remained deeply involved with and supportive of her husband's work. When he became editor of the influential *Art Journal,* she worked with him, both as helpmate and contributor. Together they published their famous topographical book *Ireland, its Scenery, Character, etc.* for which they toured the country four times. Hall was clearly appreciative of his wife's devotion and in a beautiful tribute to her on her eighty-first birthday, he wrote, 'You have been to me a guide, a companion, a friend, a wife, from that day to this, ever true, faithful, fond, devoted, my helper in many ways . . . God Bless you, my soul's darling, more the love of my youth, the love of my age, more beautiful in my sight than you were fifty years ago'. Mrs. Hall died three weeks later.

The portrait was painted when Mrs. Hall was fifty-seven and indicates something of her upright, determined character, the model wife and modern Victorian woman.

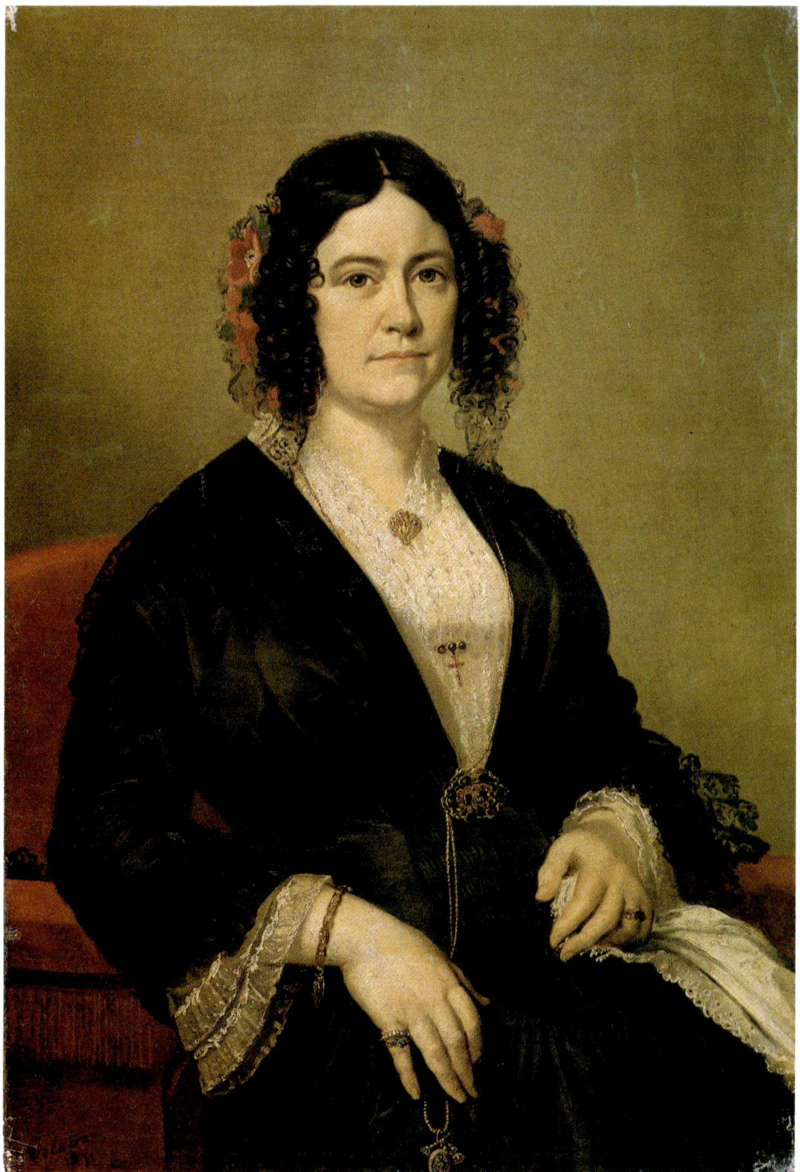

G. de Latre, 19th Century
Portrait of **MRS. SAMUEL CARTER HALL** (née Fielding),
1800-1881, Writer. Signed and dated: *de Latre, 1851*
Oil on canvas, 88 x 61 cms. Purchased, 1924

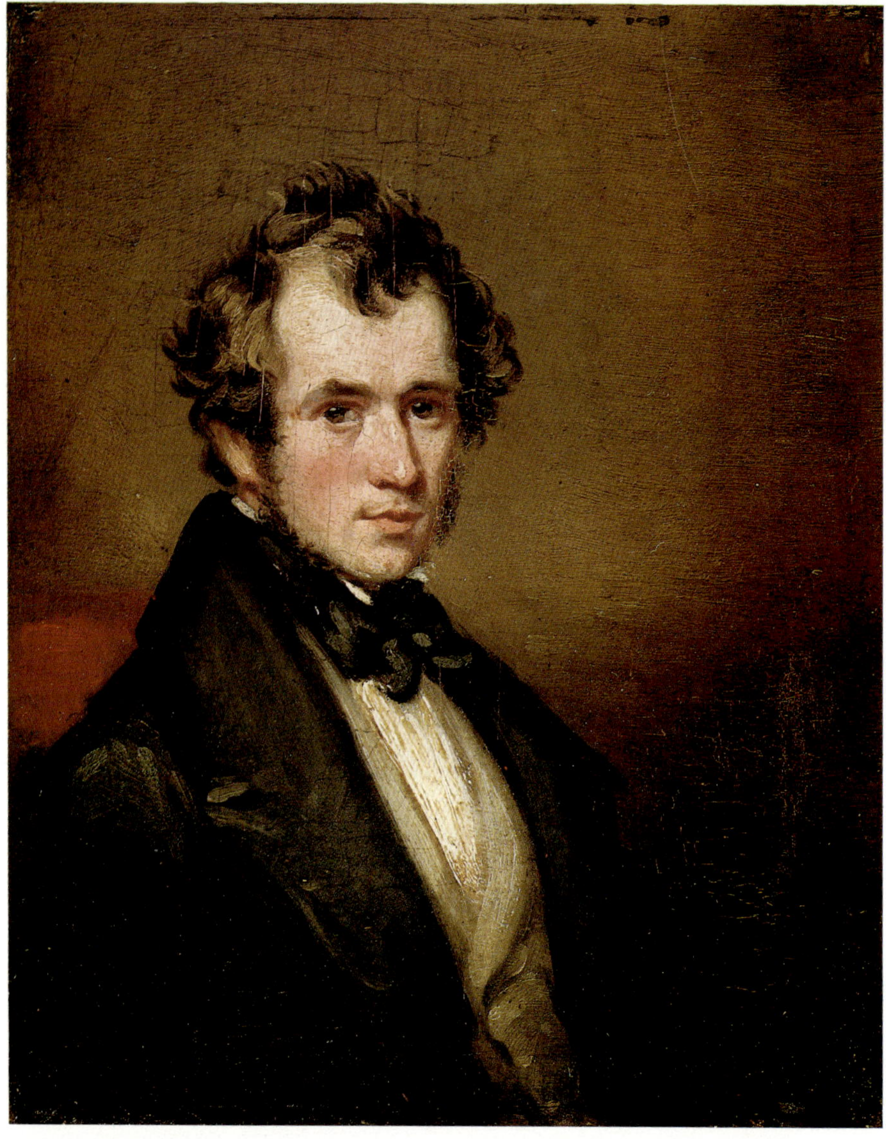

Richard Rothwell, 1780-1868
Portrait of **GERALD GRIFFIN**, 1803-1840, Poet and Novelist
Oil on panel, 168 x 102 cms. Purchased, 1910

Gerald Griffin was born in 1803 in Limerick. He was the ninth child of a poor family and when his parents emigrated to America, he was left in the care of an older brother. His first literary attempts were in poetry and journalism until John Banim (q.v.) advised him to try writing fiction. Although he had considerable success with his first collection of stories, *Holland Tide,* and with later works, Griffin studied law in order to escape the 'crushing poverty of literature'. His most famous book *The Collegians* was published anonymously, but was so popular it went into many editions. He suffered from chronic ill health and a few years before his death, he gave up writing, burned his manuscripts, and joined the Christian Brothers.

The Collegians was based on the story of a young Limerick girl named Eily Hanley, who eloped with a local squire. Her battered body was picked out of the Shannon two months later and the subsequent trial of her murderers, Jack Scanlon and his servant Stephen Sullivan, excited considerable public interest, not least because the defending council was Daniel O'Connell. As a young reporter Griffin had covered Scanlon's trial, and used the story in his novel many years later. *The Collegians* inspired Boucicault to write his play *The Colleen Bawn* and Benedict to write his opera *The Lily of Killarney.*

The artist William Rothwell could have succeeded his teacher, Sir Thomas Lawrence, as one of the most fashionable portrait painters in London, but his genius took him to Italy to study the Masters. On his return to London Rothwell neglected portaits for unsuccessful and grandiose history paintings. Griffin was probably painted by him while they were both in London about the year 1829.

The Irish composer Michael William Balfe gave his first public concert at the age of eight in his native Dublin when he appeared at the Royal Exchange as a youthful singer, composer and violinist. His father's early death left the family without a breadwinner and at sixteeen Balfe moved to London where he supported himself and his mother by playing violin in the Drury Lane Orchestra as he struggled to study composition and singing. A Russian Count, seeing in him a likeness to a dead son, became his patron and took him to Italy to further his studies.

It did not take Balfe long to establish himself as a composer of opera and as a singer. Cherubini offered to teach him composition and Rossini chose him to sing Figaro in the Paris production of *The Barber of Seville.* After a few seasons in Paris, Balfe settled in London and wrote a succession of highly popular operettas paying frequent visits to France and the opera houses of Europe where his fine tenor voice was in demand. In London he founded the English Opera Company but this was not a financial success and did not last long. He wrote over thirty operettas but is probably best remembered today as a composer of *The Bohemian Girl.*

This portrait of Balfe shows him wearing vaguely 'Bohemian' costume as if dressed for one of his operatic roles. The artist, John Wood, was an English painter who specialised in historical subjects, and as a regular exhibitor at the Royal Academy and other exhibitions. When the painting was acquired by the Gallery in 1888 Mrs. Balfe presented several manuscripts, notes and letters by Balfe and a sheet of music from his last opera, *Knight of the Leopard* based on Scott's *The Talisman.*

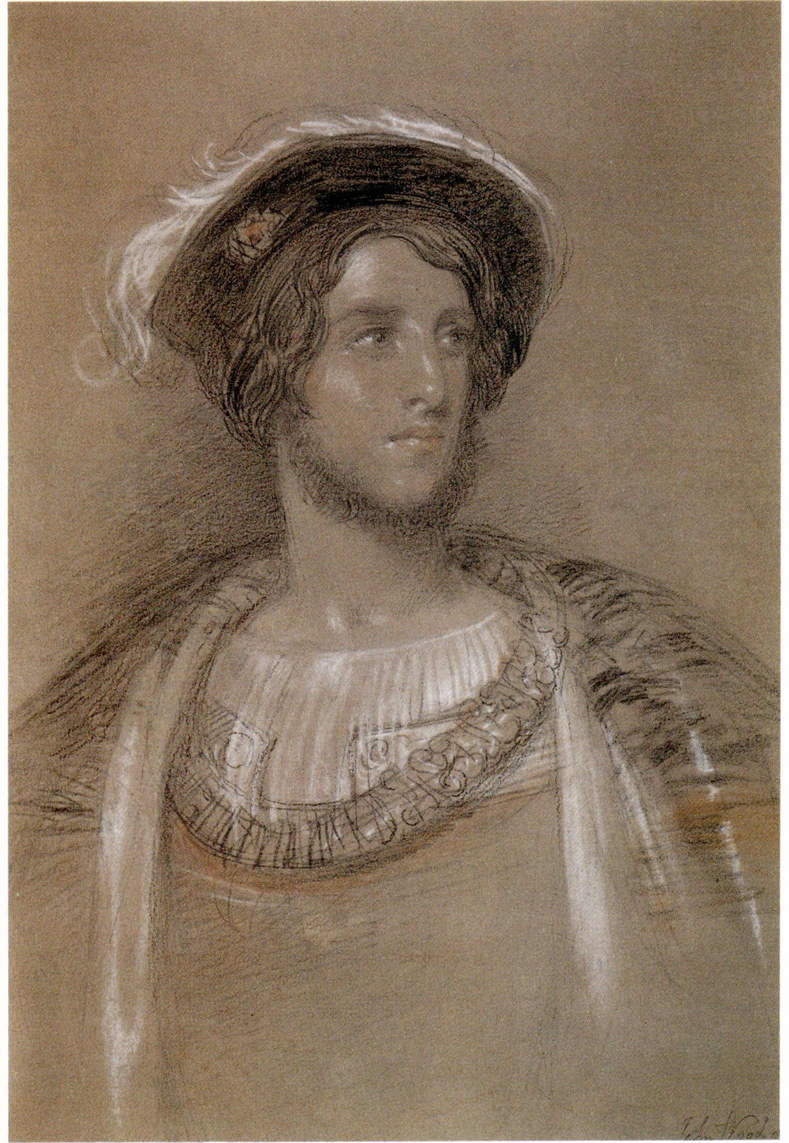

John Wood, 1801-1870
Portrait of **MICHAEL WILLIAM BALFE,** 1808-1870,
Composer and Singer. Signed: *John Wood delt.*
Red chalk and charcoal with white highlights on paper, 33.3 x 24.5 cms.
Purchased, 1889

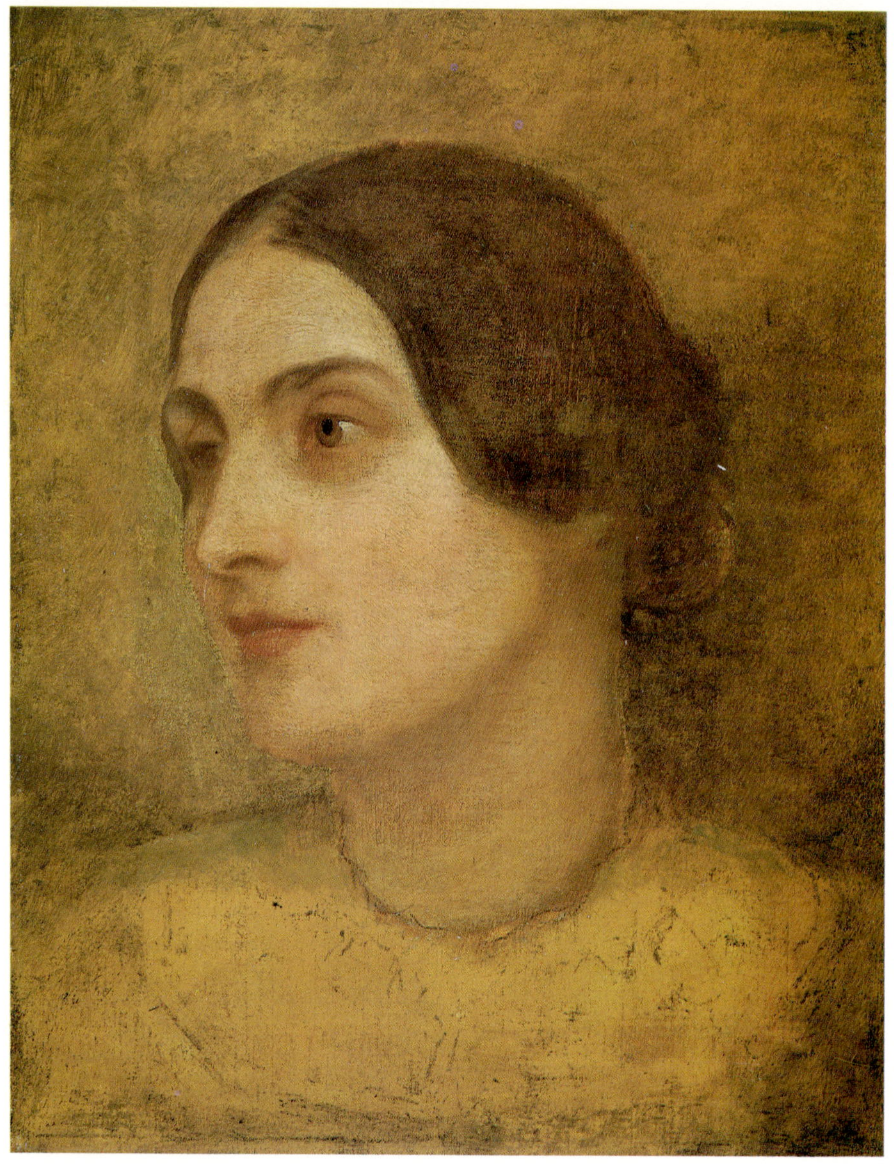

George Watts, 1817-1904
Portrait of **MRS. CAROLINE NORTON,** (née Caroline Sheridan),
1808-1877. Poet and Novelist
Oil on canvas, 42 x 33 cms. Presented by Mr. J. Ross, 1887

Caroline Norton was yet another literary member of the Sheridan family. She was born in London and raised at Hampton Court where the family was given apartments after the death of her father, Thomas Sheridan. Her mother was a popular novelist and with such a background it was no surprise that Caroline published her first book *The Dandies Rout* at the age of thirteen. Her sisters, Helena and Georgina, also became writers and these three Sheridan girls were as remarkable for their beauty as for their intellectual gifts. Caroline was the most prolific of the trio and wrote poetry and novels which were very successful in her lifetime, although little remembered today.

In 1836 Caroline's husband brought a divorce case against her, citing Lord Melbourne as co-respondent. The case failed miserably, but Mr. Norton chose to deprive his — completely vindicated — wife of access to her children until one of them died. He later claimed her considerable literary earnings as his own while refusing to support her in any way. The spirited Mrs. Norton responded with a vigorous campaign to establish women's rights to custody of children and private property, and there is little doubt that her writings went a long way towards improving the lot of women before the law in Victorian Britain.

George Frederick Watts was an English artist who earned his living as a portrait painter, but in the pursuit of greater artistic aims he painted large allegorical works and tried to revive the art of fresco painting. As part of a series of famous celebrities and beauties, he painted Mrs. Norton in 1850 at the house of a friend. He never finished the work and later she wrote of it 'The head of me is much flattered but a beautiful thing. I am sorry not to have sat more.'

Joseph Sheridan Le Fanu could claim descent from two Irish literary families; the scholarly Le Fanus and the brilliant and multi-talented Sheridan family from whom he took one of his names. Born in Dublin where his father was a clergyman, Le Fanu entered Trinity College to study law and, while still an undergraduate, he began to contribute articles to the newly founded *Dublin University Magazine.* He continued a close relationship with the magazine throughout his life, becoming in time editor and proprietor as well as contributor. He also purchased three Dublin newspapers which he amalgamated into the *Evening Mail* with a weekly supplement called *The Warder.*

When his wife died in 1858, Le Fanu seemed to undergo something of a personality change. From being a socially popular and gregarious man he became a recluse, shunning public life, and embarked on a series of Gothic novels and stories of the supernatural. He composed his macabre stories sitting in his bed, scribbling them in pencil on scraps of paper. For fifteen years he wrote stories such as *In a Glass Darkly, Uncle Silas,* and his *Ghost Stories and Tales of Mystery.* He died at his house in Merrion Square, Dublin a few days after completing his final work *Willing to Die.*

This painting of Le Fanu was executed by his son, Brindsley Sheridan Le Fanu, and was presented to the Gallery after his death. Although the Le Fanu family considered the portrait to be a good likeness of the author, it is signed and dated 1916 which suggests that it was painted posthumously and might have been copied from an earlier photograph.

Brindsley Le Fanu, 20th Century
Portrait of **JOSEPH SHERIDAN LE FANU,** 1814-1873, Writer and Journalist.
Signed and dated: *B. Le Fanu, 1916.* Oil on canvas, 36 x 26 cms.
Presented by Mr. T. Le Fanu, 1929.

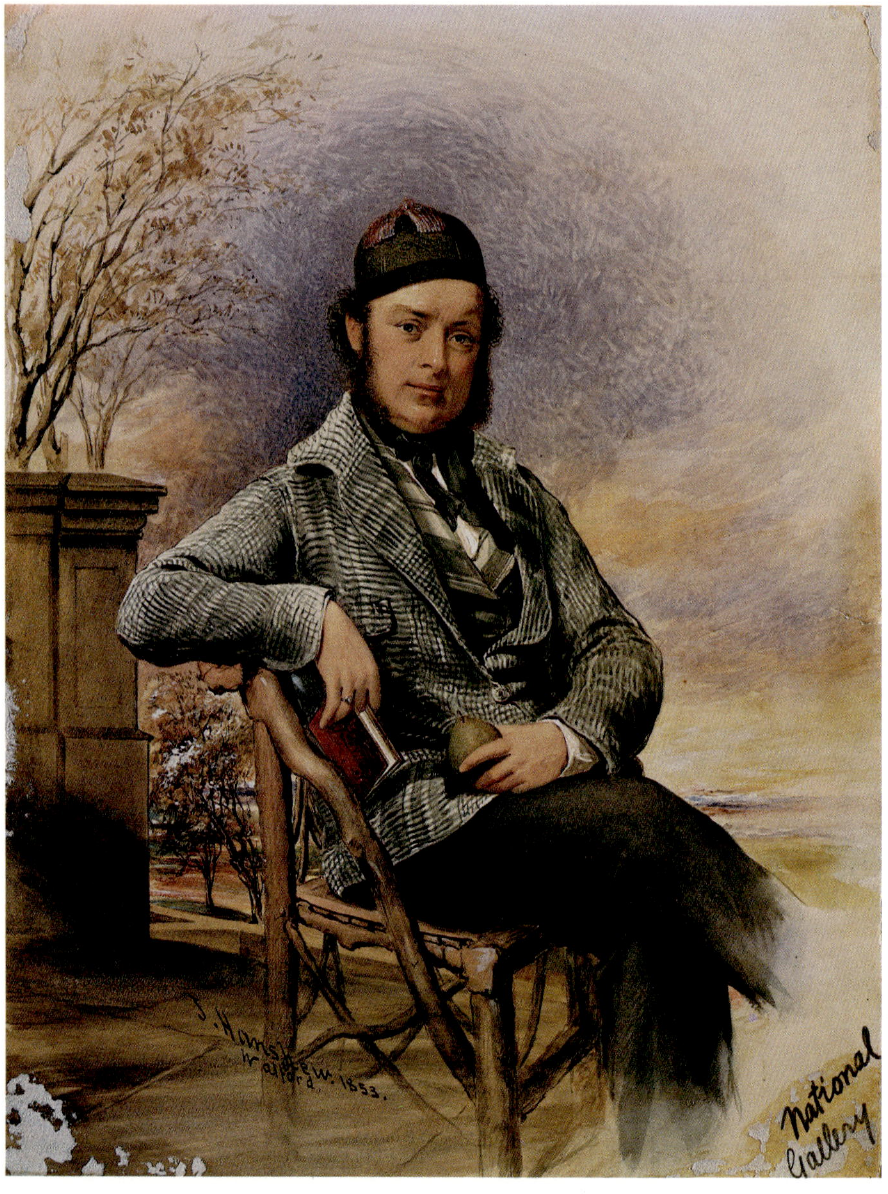

William Vincent Wallace was born in Waterford and, being musically gifted, by the age of twenty had established himself as a successful violinist in Dublin. Tiring of a conventional life, he married and set off for the Australian bush to try his hand at sheep farming. He soon abandoned both wife and sheep to the bush and set off again in search of his fortune. His life now took on the dimensions of a *Boys Own* adventure story. While whaling in New Zealand he narrowly escaped death in a mutiny; in Tasmania he was captured by natives and his life was saved by the chief's daughter; in India he was befriended by the Begum of Oude; in South America he amassed a fortune from giving concerts, and he became a bankrupt in North America through ill-judged investments.

Wallace finally returned to Europe and resumed the life of a musician. He travelled constantly, · composing and playing his own music. One of his operas *Maritana* enjoyed wide popularity and is probably the work by which he is best remembered today. However, he was a prolific composer of piano music which he performed with his second wife (bigamously married) who was a pianist. He died in the French Pyrenees at the age of 52 leaving his wife and two children in financial straits.

J. Hanshew was an English artist and in this portrait of Wallace shows him sitting at his ease on a garden seat, wearing a smoking cap and holding a book and a pear. The painting is dated 1853, when the composer was forty and after he had returned to live in Europe.

J. Hanshew, fl. c.1850
Portrait of **WILLIAM VINCENT WALLACE,** 1812-1865, Composer
Signed and dated: *J. Hanshew, 1853, Watford*
Watercolour on paper, 60. 7 x 47 cms. Purchased, 1903

Frederick William Burton was born at Corofin House, County Clare and studied art in Dublin under Robert West and the Brocas Brothers. Despite a childhood injury which disabled his right arm, Burton began to establish himself as a portrait painter in water-colour and miniature. George Petrie befriended him, attracted, according to one story, as much by his personal beauty as by his talent as an artist, and the two shared a lifelong enthusiasm for Irish antiquities and folklore. Together the two artists travelled in the West of Ireland, where Burton painted land-scapes and scenes of peasant life such as his famous *Aran Fisherman's drowned Child.* He spent several years studying and painting in Germany and his later work shows this influence. He was Director of the National Gallery in London for twenty years and was knighted in 1884.

When Gladstone appointed Burton Director of the National Gallery in 1873, the artist immediately abandoned painting, leaving unfinished works in his studio, and devoted himself com-pletely to the post. Among the many masterpieces he added to the collection are Leonardo's *Virgin of the Rocks,* Botticelli's *Venus and Mars,* and Raphael's *Ansi dei Madonna.* He would appear at public auctions to bid personally for Gallery works and dealers refrained from bidding against him. When a painting was knocked down to the National Gallery, the sale room would resound with applause.

This early portrait of Burton was fittingly painted by the first Director of the National Gallery of Ireland, George F. Mulvany. A member of an artistic Dublin family, he succeeded his father as Keeper of the Royal Hibernian Academy. He was largely responsible for the establishment of the National Gallery of Ireland.

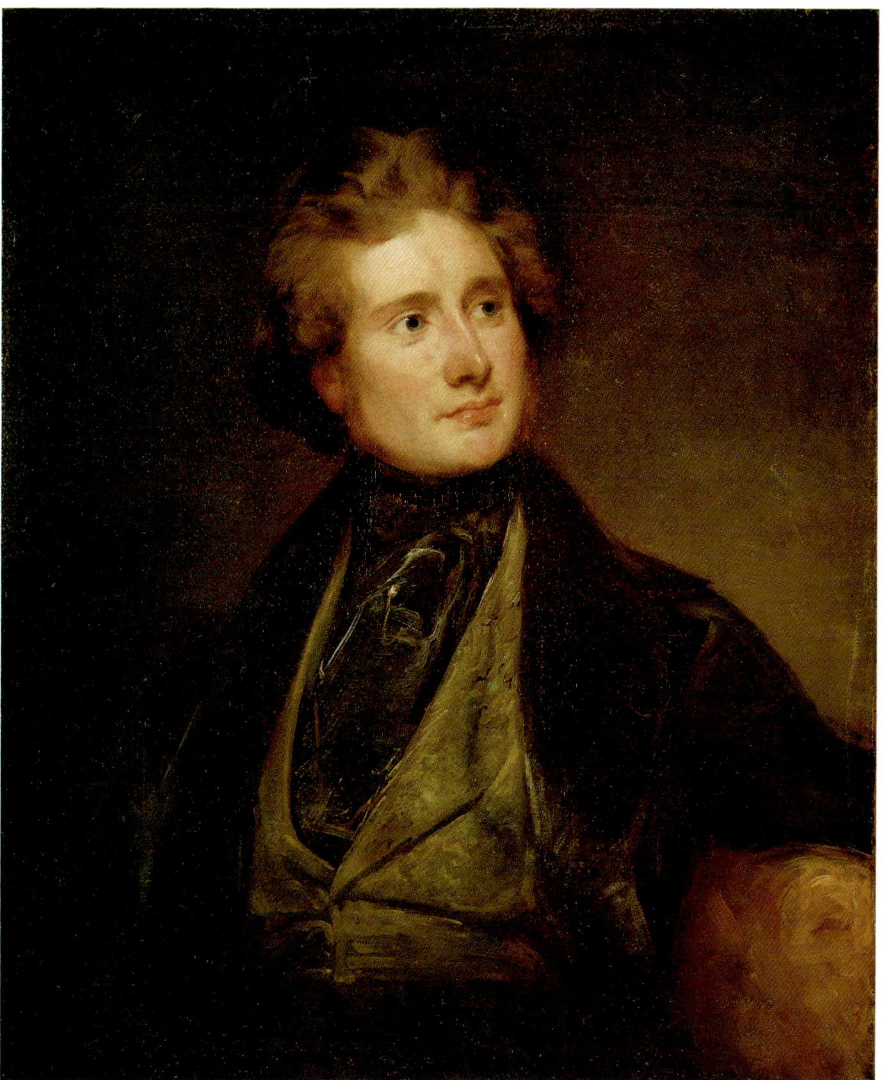

George Francis Mulvany, 1809-1869
Portrait of **FREDERICK WILLIAM BURTON**, 1816-1900, Artist
Oil on canvas, 74 x 61 cms. Purchased, 1892

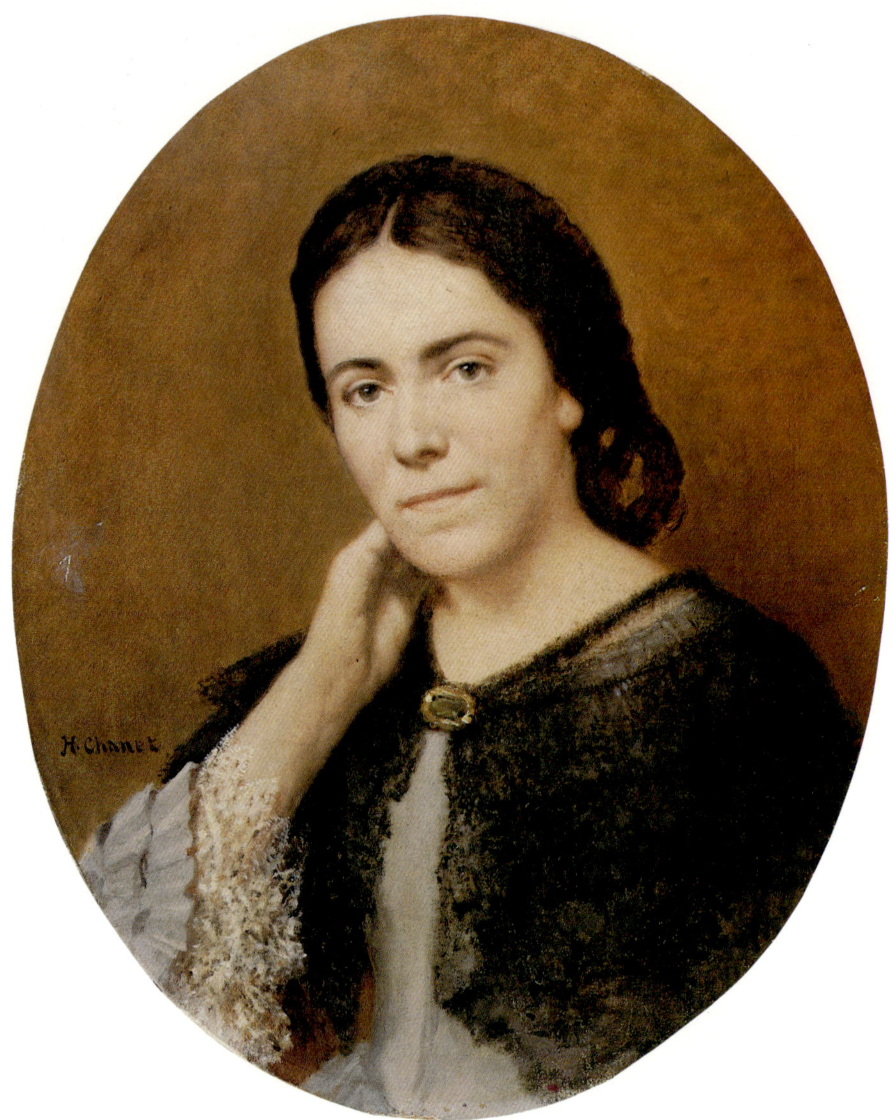

Julia Kavanagh was the only child of a now forgotten Victorian romantic poet and novelist, Morgan Peter Kavanagh. Although she was born in Thurles, County Tipperary, most of her life was spent in France. She began to earn her living from journalism and her first novel, a children's book entitled *The Three Natts,* was published when she was 23. She also published a series of biographical essays of high moral tone about women of character such as *Woman of Christianity exemplyfying acts of Piety and Charity.* She quarrelled with her father when he claimed her collaboration in one of his own works.

Although so little of her life was passed in Ireland, Julia Kavanagh had no doubts about her origins. She wrote to Gavan Duffy offering to contribute to *The Nation.* 'I am Irish by origin, birth and feeling, though not by education, but if I have lived far from Ireland she has still been as the faith and religion of my youth'. She was prepared to put her pen at the service of the paper for no other reward than the interests of her country.

Julia Kavanagh died suddenly in Nice after falling out of bed at the age of 53. She was survived by the invalid mother she had cared for all her life. Mrs. Kavanagh presented this portrait to the Gallery a few years after her daughter's death. The work is by a French Academic artist and was probably painted while she lived in Paris. It was exhibited at the Paris Salon and the Royal Academy in London in 1883.

Henri Chanet, fl. after 1874
Portrait of **JULIA KAVANAGH**, 1824-1877, Author
Signed: *H. Chanet.* Oil on canvas, 53 x 49 cms.
Presented by Mrs. M. Kavanagh, 1884

As a young woman embued with nationalistic fervour, Jane Francesca Elgee (better known to the world by her married name, Lady Wilde), contributed rousing patriotic verse to *The Nation* under the pseudonym 'Speranza'. The paper was suppressed for sedition and during the trial of the editor, Charles Gavan Duffy, Miss Elgee rose dramatically in court to claim authorship of the inflammatory article which had caused the closure. After her marriage to the Dublin surgeon and antiquarian, Sir William Wilde, her interests turned to literature and the collecting of Irish folklore.

The Wilde's home in Merrion Square, Dublin was the centre of a literary circle and here Speranza received her guests with curtains drawn, even in daylight, dressed flamboyantly, heavily bejewelled, her striking figure posed in the role of Literary Genius. 'The State,' she wrote prophetically, 'surely ought to consider the importance of preserving genius from low care, and Parliament might pass a bill to exempt the race of the gifted from taxation'. Lady Wilde's later years were shadowed by the public disgrace of both husband and son. She moved to London after her husband's death, and bravely tried to continue her literary salon, although in very straitened circumstances. She died while her son Oscar served his time in Reading Gaol.

This drawing was bought in Dublin in 1959. It is an unsual drawing of Lady Wilde of whom few portraits exist, and was probably a caricature for a magazine. It shows her as guests might have found her entertaining at No 1, Merrion Square, wearing a gilded laurel wreath and bizarre jewellery.

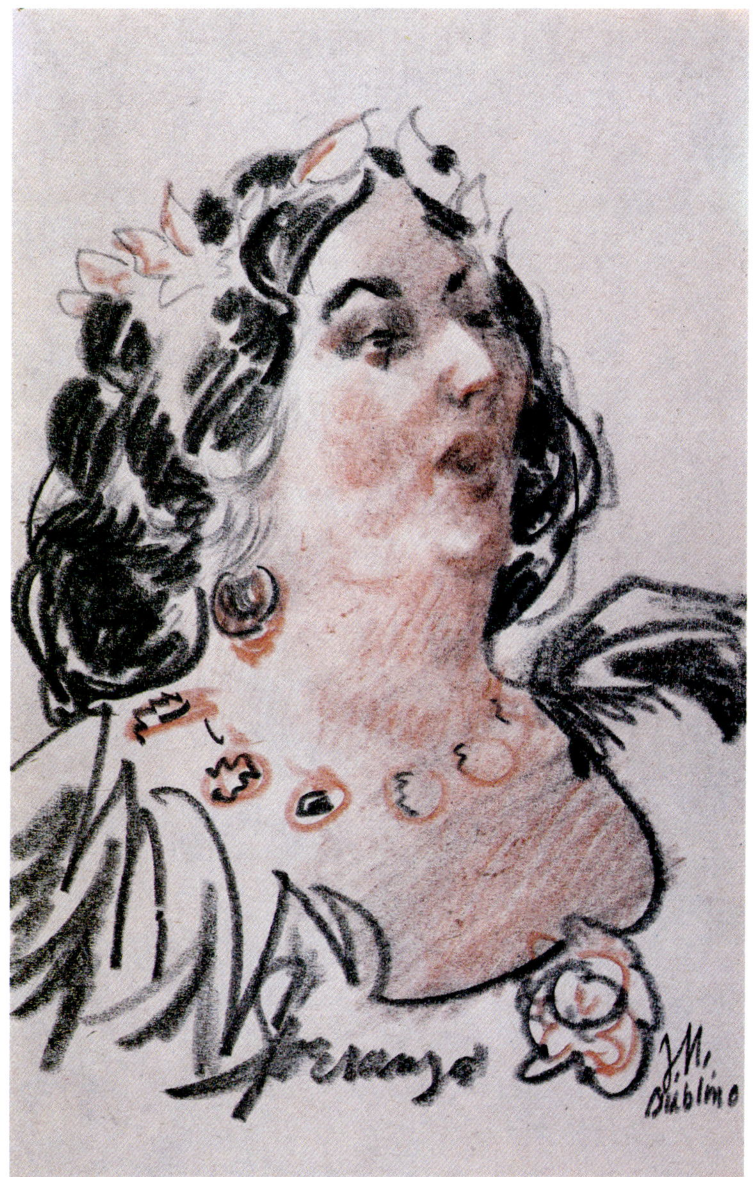

John Hughes, (1865-1941) attributed to
Portrait of **LADY WILDE**, 1826-1896, Writer (pen-name Speranza)
Signed: *JH Dublino*
Crayon on paper, 19 x 12.4 cms. Purchased, 1967

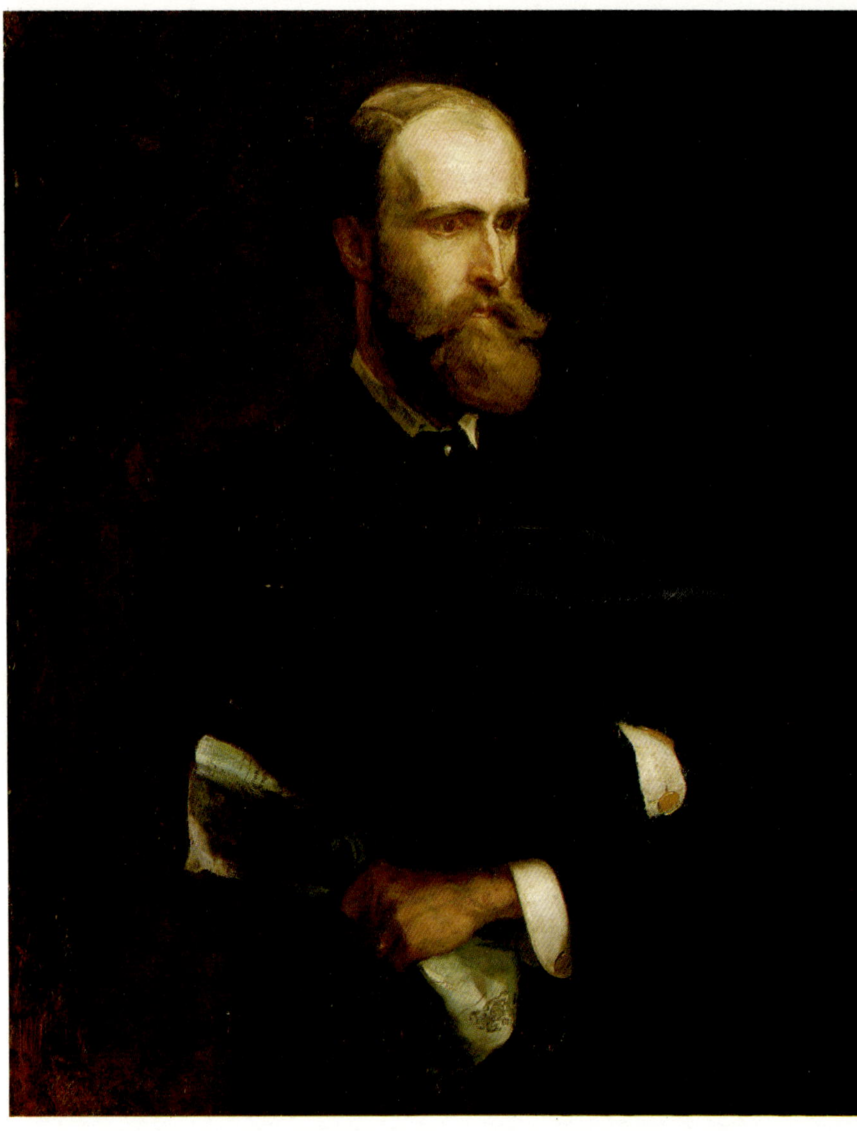

Sydney Prior Hall, 1842-1922
Portrait of **CHARLES STEWART PARNELL,** 1846-1891, Statesman
Signed and dated: *S.P. Hall, 1892*
Oil on canvas, 112 x 86 cms. Presented by Sir John Brunner, 1898

Few Irish leaders have attracted so much adulation and hatred as Charles Stewart Parnell. Born at Avondale, County Wicklow, into a family with a tradition of political service, Parnell entered Parliament as M.P. for Meath and joined the Home Rule party. He employed Biggar's obstruction tactics in Parliament to get good effect and became President of the National Land League. During the Land War of 1872-1882, Parnell's was the most powerful voice in the country while organized boycotting and private courts overturned English law. The elections of 1883 and 1885 saw Parnell as undisputed 'Chief'. An attempt to discredit him with the forged Pigott letters failed and he was cleared by the Parnell Commission in 1890. He was now at the peak of his career.

The year Parnell was acquitted by the Commission, he was cited as co-respondent in a divorce case. His relationship with Mrs. Kitty O'Shea had been known for many years, but Captain O'Shea now decided to use it to discredit his former political colleague. Parnell refused to contest the case and a wave of public outrage swept the country and the sensitive Irish morality was deeply offended by the private life of its revered leader. His career was shattered and Gladstone had no recourse but to demand his resignation. Parnell retired to Avondale, married Kitty O'Shea and died three years later.

Sidney Prior Hall was an English illustrator and war artist who covered the Parnell Commission for *The Graphic* and later painted this oil portrait of Parnell. Hall wrote 'Mr. Parnell never consciously sat for me, but I sketched him for many hours in all sorts of poses during the Commission. I meant the pose to suggest Parnell's defiant attitude in the House of Commons, where I had also sketched him'.

Born on his family estate, Moore Park, at Ballyglass, County Mayo, George Moore received little education or training for life. He was raised a Catholic and at one time prepared for the priesthood, but later rejected all religion. When his father died he went to Paris to study art and although he soon realized his talent in this field was limited, he remained there enjoying café life and friendship with Degas, Fromentin, Picasso and other artists. When the family estate finally ceased to support his dilettante existence, Moore turned in earnest to literature to support himself. His first novel, published in London in 1883, had a modest success and earned him a place among modern novelists. By the time he moved to Dublin in 1901, fired by the enthusiasm of his cousin, Edward Martyn, for the Irish Literary Renaissance, Moore was already an established literary figure.

In Dublin Moore argued with Yeats (q.v.), Martyn and Russell, wrote plays in French for translation into Irish, encouraged everyone to learn Irish except himself, and helped found the Irish Literary Theatre. After ten exhausting years of enthusiasm he left Ireland, returning to live in London, and recounted his Irish experiences in his witty, amusing and very successful three volume autobiograhy *Hail and Fairwell.*

John Butler Yeats was a fine portrait painter but a very slow worker. His portrait of Moore was commissioned by the New-York millionaire John Quinn in 1910. Lily Yeats wrote to Quinn of the painting's slow progress, and described it as a very good portrait that did not make people laugh at Moore the way most portraits did. John Yeats spent almost a year working on the portrait until Moore tired of sitting for it and left Ireland before it was completed.

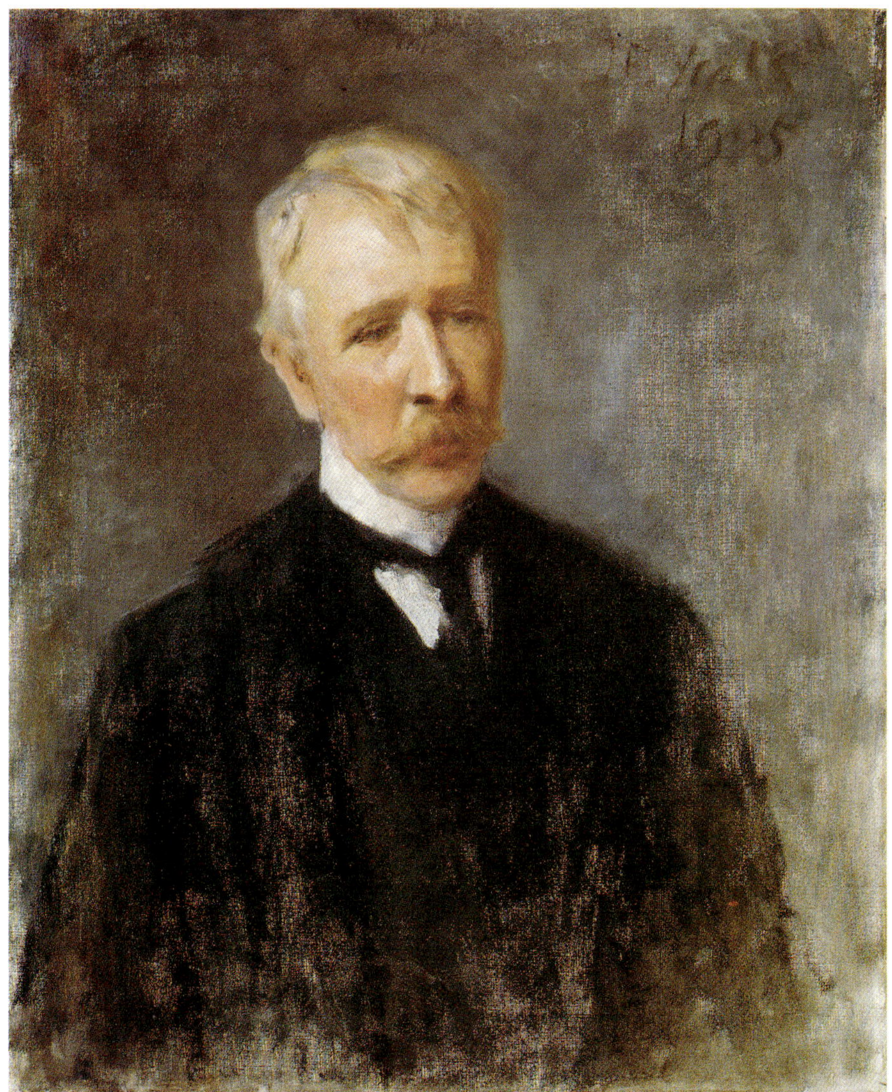

John Butler Yeats, 1839-1922
Portrait of **GEORGE MOORE,** 1852-1933, Novelist
Oil on canvas, 77 x 64 cms. Presented by Mr. C. Sullivan in memory of Mr. J. Quinn, 1926

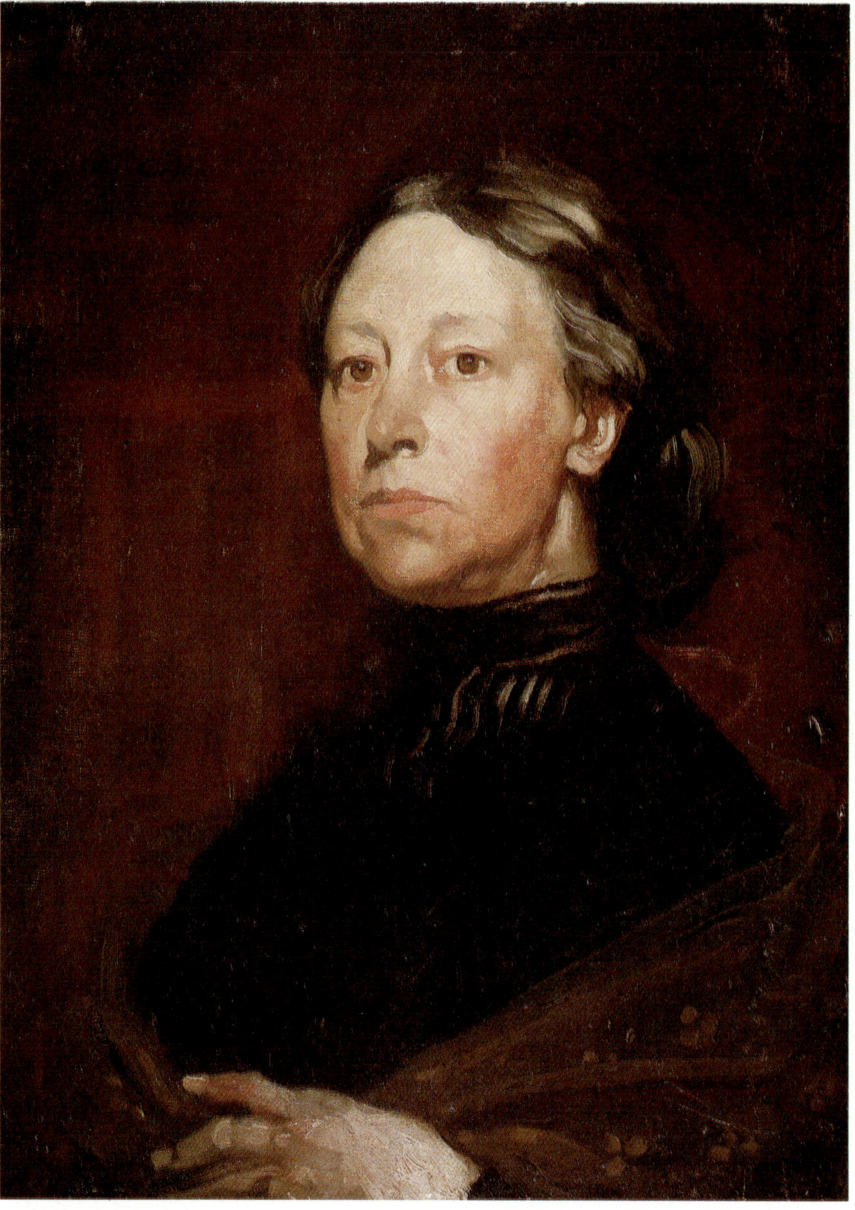

William Orpen, 1878-1931
Portrait of **AUGUSTA GREGORY**, 1852-1932, Dramatist
Oil on canvas, 61 x 46 cms. Purchased, 1953

Lady Gregory was born into a landowning family in Roxborough, County Galway. She married the owner of Coole Park estate, Sir Wiliam Gregory, a neighbour and a widower many years her senior. She shared his interest in politics and the arts, and edited his autobiography after his death. A chance meeting with W.B. Yeats (q.v.) turned Lady Gregory's attention to the collection of local folklore, and to Coole Park she welcomed many of the famous literary figures of her time including Moore (q.v.), Martyn, Hyde, Yeats (q.v.) and Synge. These gatherings led to the creation of the Irish Literary Theatre which opened in Dublin in 1899. When the Abbey Theatre was founded in 1904, Lady Gregory became co-director with Yeats and Synge and took to writing plays in an attempt to provide the company with material. She wrote forty plays over the next twenty-five years.

Lady Gregory was a keen nationalist from her early days and helped Douglas Hyde found a branch of the Gaelic League at Kiltartan, near Coole. She learned Irish, and her interest in peasant dialect led her to invent her own dramatic dialogue which she called 'Kilternan', and into this she translated French plays and transcribed folk-stories. Although the attempt was unwieldy, Synge was sufficiently influenced to make his own excursions into dramatic dialogue based on the speech of the West of Ireland.

This forceful portrait by William Orpen was purchased by the Gallery from the artist's widow. Orpen was a successful portrait painter and a friend of Sir Hugh Lane, who commissioned him to finish the series begun by John Butler Yeats of Irish Personalities, destined by Lane for an Irish National Portrait Gallery.

George Bernard Shaw held few happy memories of his early years in Dublin where his father was an unsuccessful merchant and his own education was sketchy. He moved to London as soon as he was able and slowly began to establish himself as a journalist. For several years he was music critic of *The Star,* writing under the pseudonym 'Corno di Basseto', and later be became one of the most influential drama critics of his day, one of the first to recognise the importance of Ibsen, and an advocate of modern drama. When he began to write plays himself they were considered very modern and rather shocking. He was one of the first Fabians and a convinced vegetarian, living to the age of ninety-four. In his long and very prolific career, Shaw wrote over fifty plays, several volumes of critical reviews and essays, and was awarded the Nobel Prize for Literature in 1925.

Shaw was undoubtedly one of the greatest benefactors the National Gallery of Ireland has ever had. In his will he left his estate to be divided equally between the British Museum, the Royal Academy of Dramatic Art in London and the National Gallery of Ireland. In 1944 he wrote to Thomas Bodkin of his intentions for the Gallery 'to which I owe much of the only education I ever got as a boy in Eire'. The success of the film *My Fair Lady,* adapted from his play *Pygmalion,* allowed the Gallery to purchase masterpieces which would otherwise have remained out of reach.

In 1925 Mrs. Shaw, ever occupied with the public image of her husband, offered this portrait to the Gallery. It had been given to her some years before by the artist John Collier, 'who is' she wrote 'even older than GBS'. She was most anxious that the painting should be hung in the Gallery during the artist's lifetime.

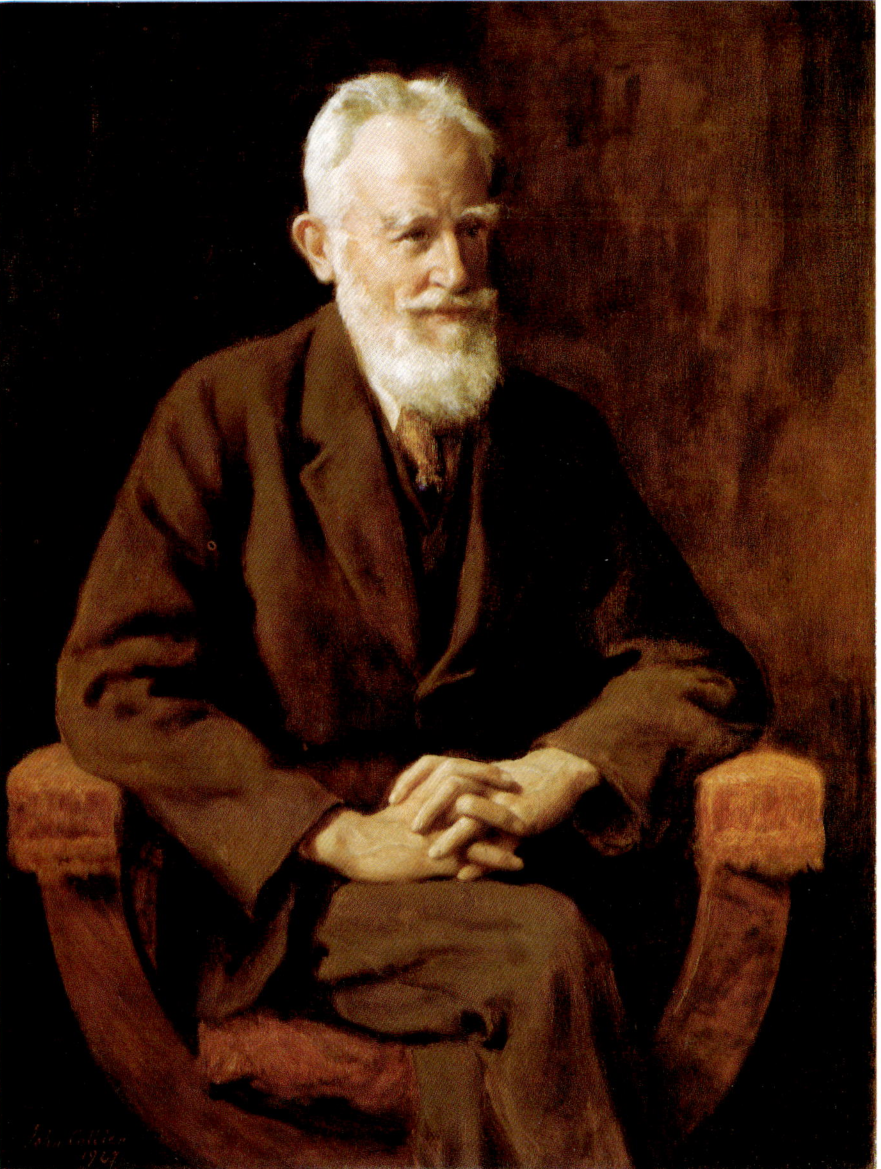

John Collier, 1850-1934
Portrait of **GEORGE BERNARD SHAW**, 1856-1950, Dramatist
Signed and dated: *John Collier, 1927*
Oil on canvas, 112 x 86 cms. Presented by Mrs. B. Shaw, 1928

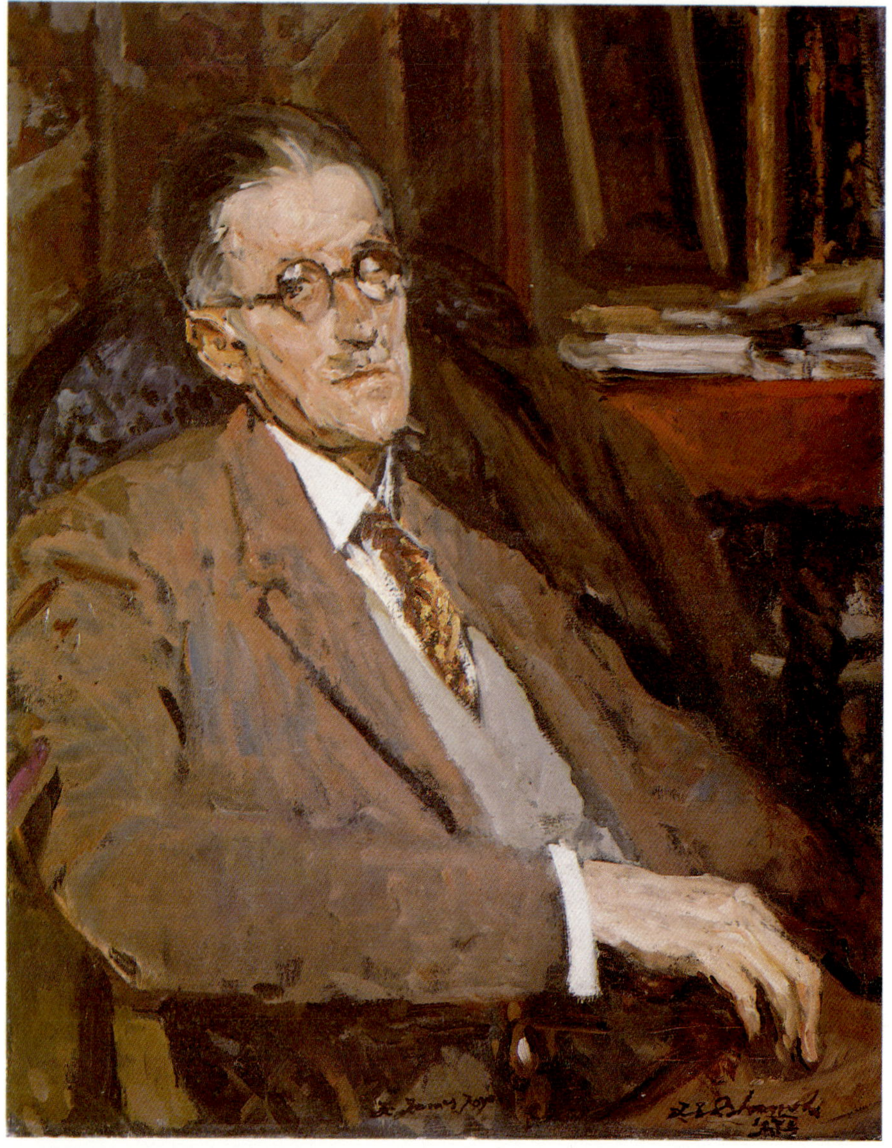

Jacques-Emile Blanche, 1861-1942
Portrait of **JAMES JOYCE,** 1882-1941, Author
Signed and dated: *J.E. Blanche, 1934*
Oil on canvas, 82 x 65 cms. Purchased, 1941

James Joyce, the novelist, was born in Dublin in 1882. He was educated at the Jesuit Colleges of Clongowes Wood and Belvedere before entering University College, Dublin to study languages. He tried to study medicine in Paris and briefly thought of making a career as a singer before devoting himself completely to literature, and his first novel *Portrait of the Artist as a Young Man* was begun while he was still a student. In 1904 Joyce left Ireland with his life long companion, the Galway born Nora Barnacle, to live on the Continent, moving between France, Italy and Switzerland. His life was a constant struggle to earn a living from writing and to have his works published. His most controversial work *Ulysses,* was banned in the United States until a court case ruled in 1934 that the book was not pornography. Joyce was in Paris when the Second World War broke out and he moved with his family to Zurich where he died in 1941.

While living in Paris, Joyce was anxious to have his portrait painted by the French artist, Émile Blanche. Joyce sat for the portrait in March 1934. He would not allow Blanche to paint him full face as he felt this would accentuate his thick lenses. He took a keen interest in the later history of the painting, although he wrote of it to his family, 'I think it's awful except for the splendid tie I had on'.

After Joyce's death the Director of the National Gallery of Ireland initiated a search for this portrait, eventually tracking it down in Paris and, despite the war, managed to buy it. Another Blanche portrait of Joyce, now in the National Portrait Gallery London, shows the writer in the same clothes — and tie — but standing with his arms crossed. This second portrait is dated 1935 and may have been painted from the original sittings.

Although born in Dublin, William Butler Yeats divided his childhood between London, where his father lived, and Sligo, where he spent summers with his mother's family. George Russell encouraged his interest in mysticism, John O'Leary introduced him to Irish mythology and Yeats soon found his own voice. 'I turned my back on foreign themes,' he wrote, 'and decided that the race was more important than the individual.' Friendship with Lady Gregory (q.v.) led to summers at Coole Park and the planning of the Irish National Theatre. When the Abbey was founded, Yeats was chief dramatist as well as director and fund raiser. He founded the Irish Academy of Letters with George Bernard Shaw (q.v.) and was awarded the Nobel Prize for Literature in 1923. He died in the South of France in 1939.

While Lady Gregory was the organizing genius of the Irish Literary Theatre, Yeats was undoubtedly the moving spirit and central guru. To his contemporaries Yeats appeared as the epitome of a 'Poet' with his tall striking figure and unconventional dress. He sank into inspirational trances, composed his poetry muttering *sotto voce,* and when he read aloud to his friends, his melodious voice, grand gestures and the burning vehemence in his eye entranced his admiring acolytes. Advised by a doctor, late in life, to avoid excitement, Yeats exclaimed 'I have lived a life of excitement'.

Edmund Dulac was a French illustrator who worked chiefly in England and was an intimate of Yeats' later years. He designed the masks for Yeats' first Noh play, and in this drawing shows his friend in the full flight of artistic inspiration. The drawing was presented by Sir Alec Martin in 1942 in memory of his long association with Yeats.

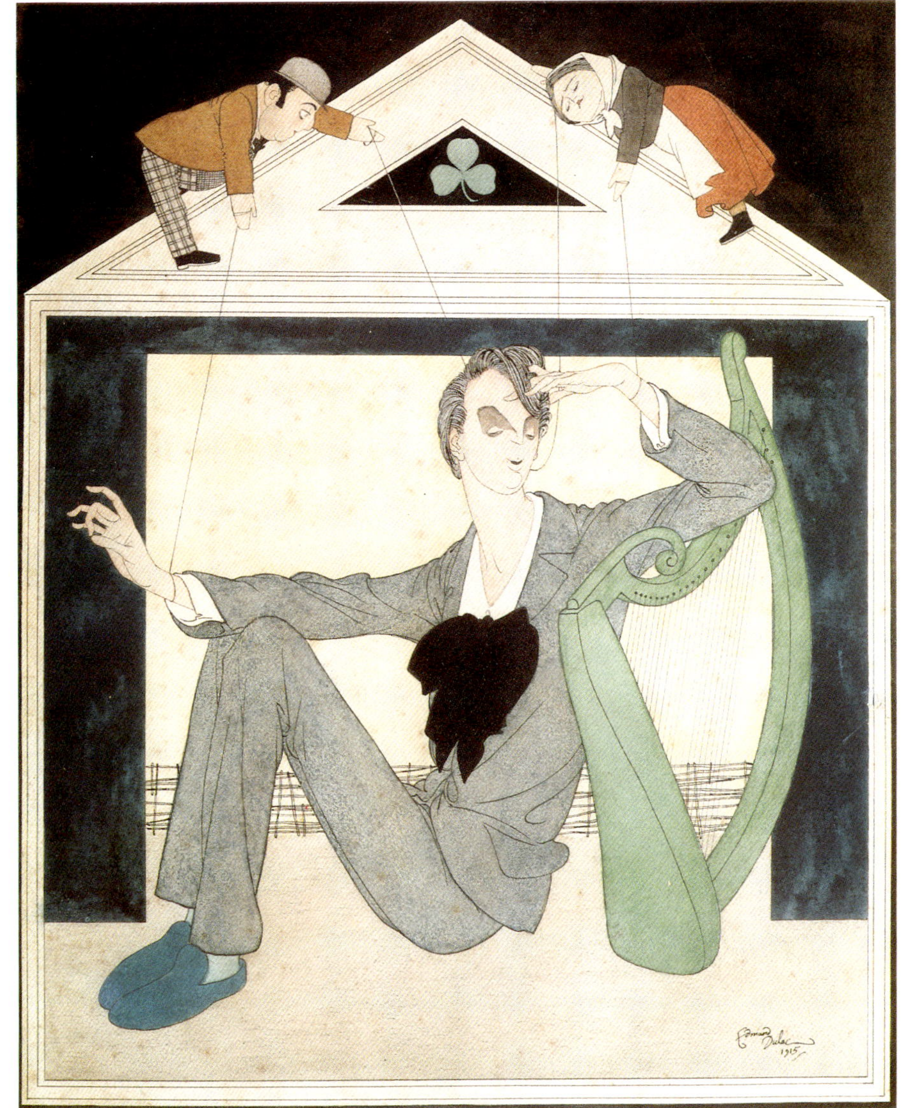

Edmund Dulac, 1882-1953
Portrait of **WILLIAM BUTLER YEATS,** 1865-1939,
Poet and Dramatist.
Signed and dated: *Edmund Dulac, 1915*
Ink, pencil and watercolour on paper, 29.1 x 35.5 cms.
Presented by Sir Alec Martin, 1942

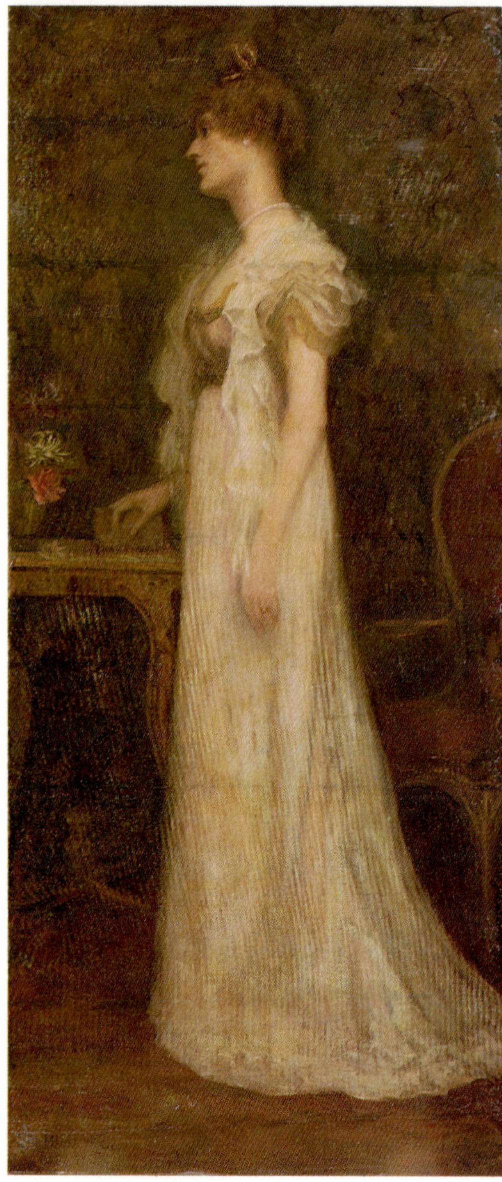

Casimir de Markievicz, fl. early 20th Century
Portrait of **CONSTANCE, COUNTESS MARKIEVICZ,**
1868-1927, Artist and Revolutionary
Oil on canvas, 205 x 91 cms. Purchased, 1952

As a young girl Constance Gore-Booth was presented to Queen Victoria and society hailed her as the new Irish Beauty. She decided to study art, first at the Slade School, London, then in Bohemian Paris. Here she met Count Markievicz-Dunin, a Polish aristocrat who had established himself as a competant portrait painter. When the Count's first wife died in 1899 they were free to marry. They moved to Dublin to live and entered fully into the artistic life of the city, becoming involved in the Abbey and founding the United Arts Club. Their only child was born at the Countess's family home at Lissadell, County Sligo.

Now Countess Markievicz turned her attention to national politics. She joined *Inghinidhe na hÉireann* and *Sinn Féin,* founded *Na Fianna Éireann* to train boys in the use of arms and ran a soup kitchen in Liberty Hall during the 1913 Lockout. In the 1916 uprising the Countess herself carried arms and fought alongside Michael Mallin at the College of Surgeons. Condemned to death for this, her sentence was commuted to life imprisonment because of her sex. The amnesty of 1917 released her and she continued her political activities throughout the Civil War and after. She was the first woman M.P. returned to Westminster, but Sinn Féin policy did not allow her to take her seat. She was a member of Dáil Éireann at her death in 1927.

Count Markievicz-Dunin painted this portrait of his wife in Paris in the year of their marriage. He continued to paint while living in Dublin, but his wife's involvement in politics drove him away and he did not return until she was mortally ill. The romantic tone of the painting presages nothing of the Countess's later military activities.

The Irish artist John Lavery first met his second wife, Hazel, in Brittany where she was on a sketching holiday with her mother. Although attracted to the widowed artist almost thirty years her senior, Hazel was already engaged to a lawyer from her native Chicago and had no thought of marrying without her parent's approval. When they next met some years later in Paris, Hazel was now also widowed with a young daughter. They married at last and the only dissenting voice was that of the five year old daughter who had hoped to marry Lavery herself when she grew up.

The Laverys lived chiefly in London where Lady Lavery's beauty and grace as a hostess drew around them a wide circle of artists and political friends. Winston Churchill, who often painted with Lavery, claimed Lady Lavery to be his first artistic inspiration. Michael Collins was a personal friend and during negotiations for the Treaty in 1921 the Laverys entertained the Irish leaders at their London home, while Lady Lavery assiduously introduced them to her English political friends in the hope of easing the talks.

John Lavery was born in Belfast and, orphaned as a child, was raised in Glasgow by relatives. He quickly established himself as a society portrait painter and many of the notables of his day sat for him. He remained very interested in the struggle for Irish Independence and often painted the Irish leaders and historical figures and events of the day, such as *Casement's Trial* and the *Signing of the Treaty*. One of his favourite subjects was his beautiful wife and in 1923 the Irish State commissioned him to paint her as Cathleen ni Houlihan for use on Irish bank notes, where she can be seen to this day as the watermark.

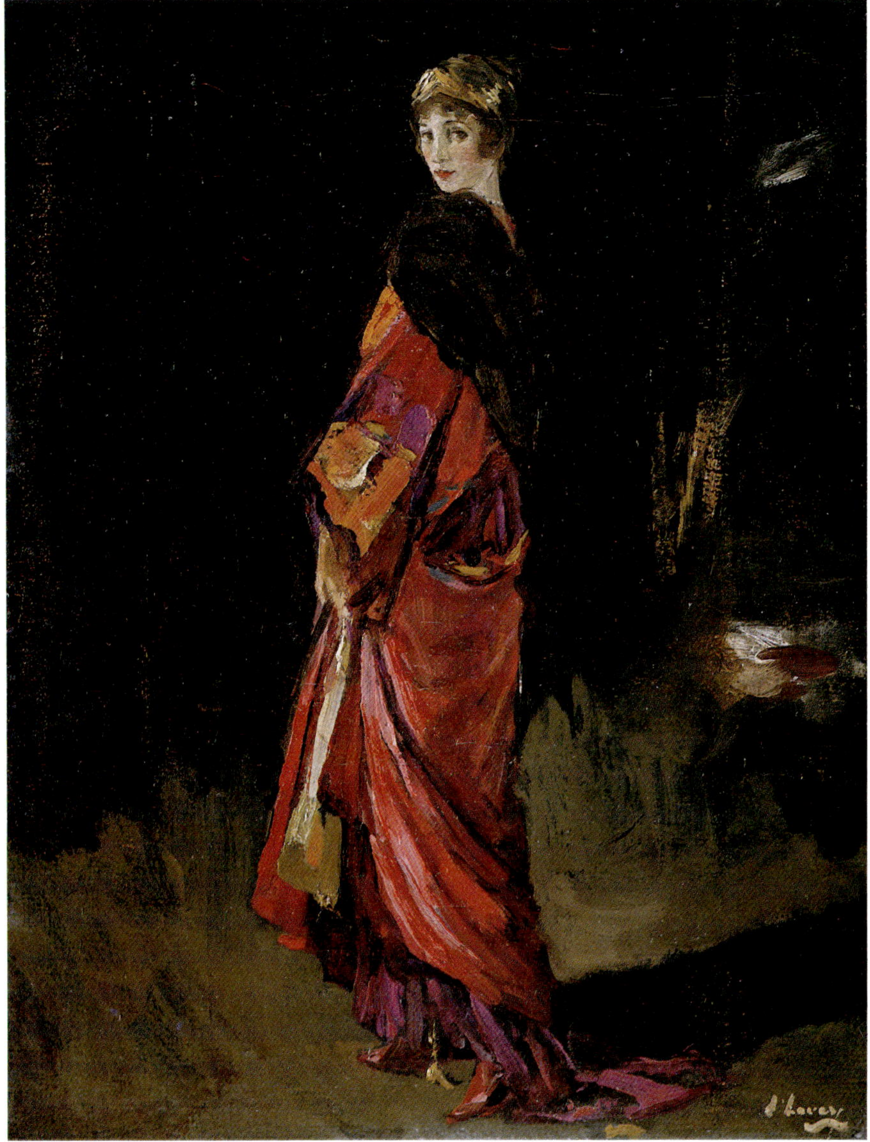

John Lavery, 1856-1941
Portrait of **LADY LAVERY,** c. 1887-1935, in an Evening Cloak
Signed: *J. Lavery*
Oil on canvas, 46 x 36 cms. Presented by the Executors of the late
Mr. E. Marsh, 1953

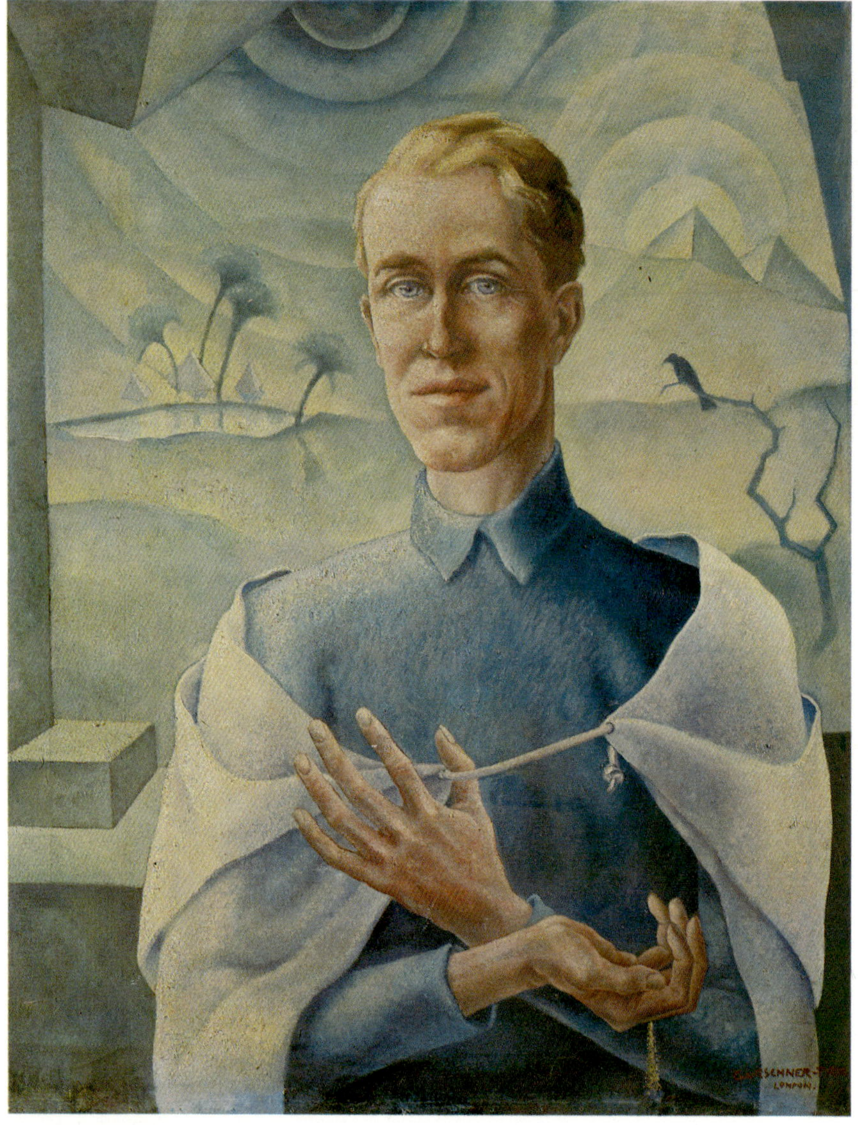

Herbert Gurschner, b. 1901
Portrait of **THOMAS EDWARD LAWRENCE** (Lawrence of Arabia),
1888-1935, Soldier and Writer
Signed: *Gurschner — Tirol London*
Oil on canvas, 97 x 76 cms.
Presented by Major D. Chapman-Huston, 1950

Thomas Edward Lawrence, better known as Lawrence of Arabia, was born in North Wales where his father, adopting the assumed name of Lawrence, had settled after leaving his legitimate Irish family. Thomas studied Ancient History at Oxford and worked as an archaeologist in the Middle East before being commissioned in the British Army on the outbreak of the First World War. His knowledge of Arab affairs and languages made him a natural choice for army intelligence work in the Middle East and he became liaison officer and adviser to King Feisal during the Arab revolt against the Turkish Empire. After the war Lawrence's promise of independence to the Arabs was not honoured by Britain and he returned to England in disillusionment. He changed his name to Shaw and enlisted in the Royal Air Force in an attempt to avoid the publicity engendered by his legendary exploits in Arabia, but controversy continued to follow him until his premature death in a motor cycle accident at the age of 47.

Lawrence's military adventures among the Arabs have been much discussed and written about, perhaps never better than in his own book *Seven Pillars of Wisdom,* published after the war, and giving his version of the Arab campaign. He wrote other books in his desire to establish a literary reputation for himself and was very pleased to be invited to join the Irish Academy of Letters on its foundation in 1932 by his friend George Bernard Shaw (q.v.), as it gave him the opportunity of publicly admitting that he was Irish.

This portrait of Lawrence was commissioned from the Austrian artist Herbert Gurschner in 1934 by a kinsman of Lawrence's father's Irish family, and was presented by him to the Gallery after Lawrence's death.

INDEX

INDEX OF PORTRAITS